Soppy

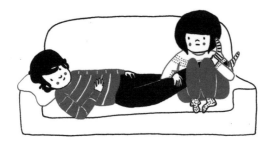

philippa Rice

Andrews McMeel
Publishing®

a division of Andrews McMeel Universal

for Luke

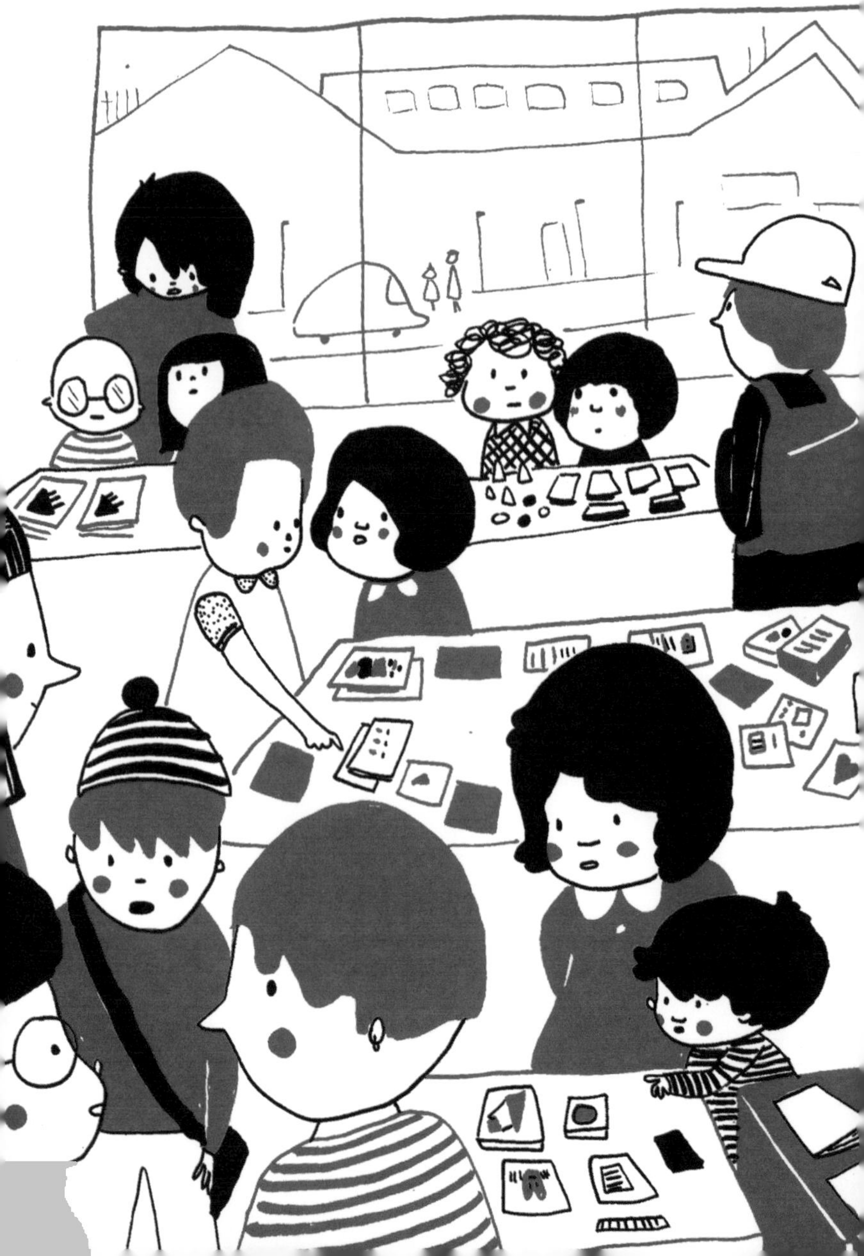

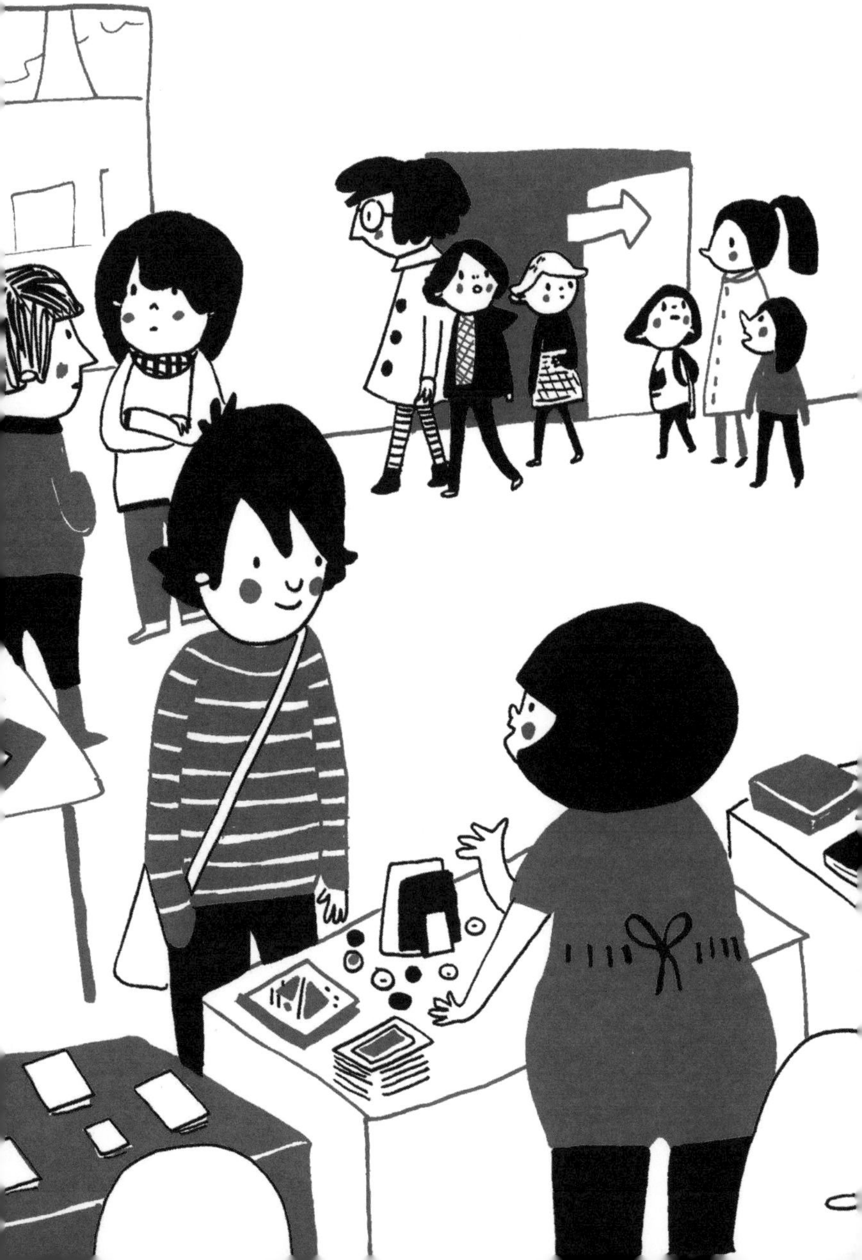

OPEN

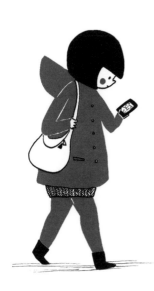

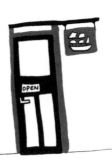

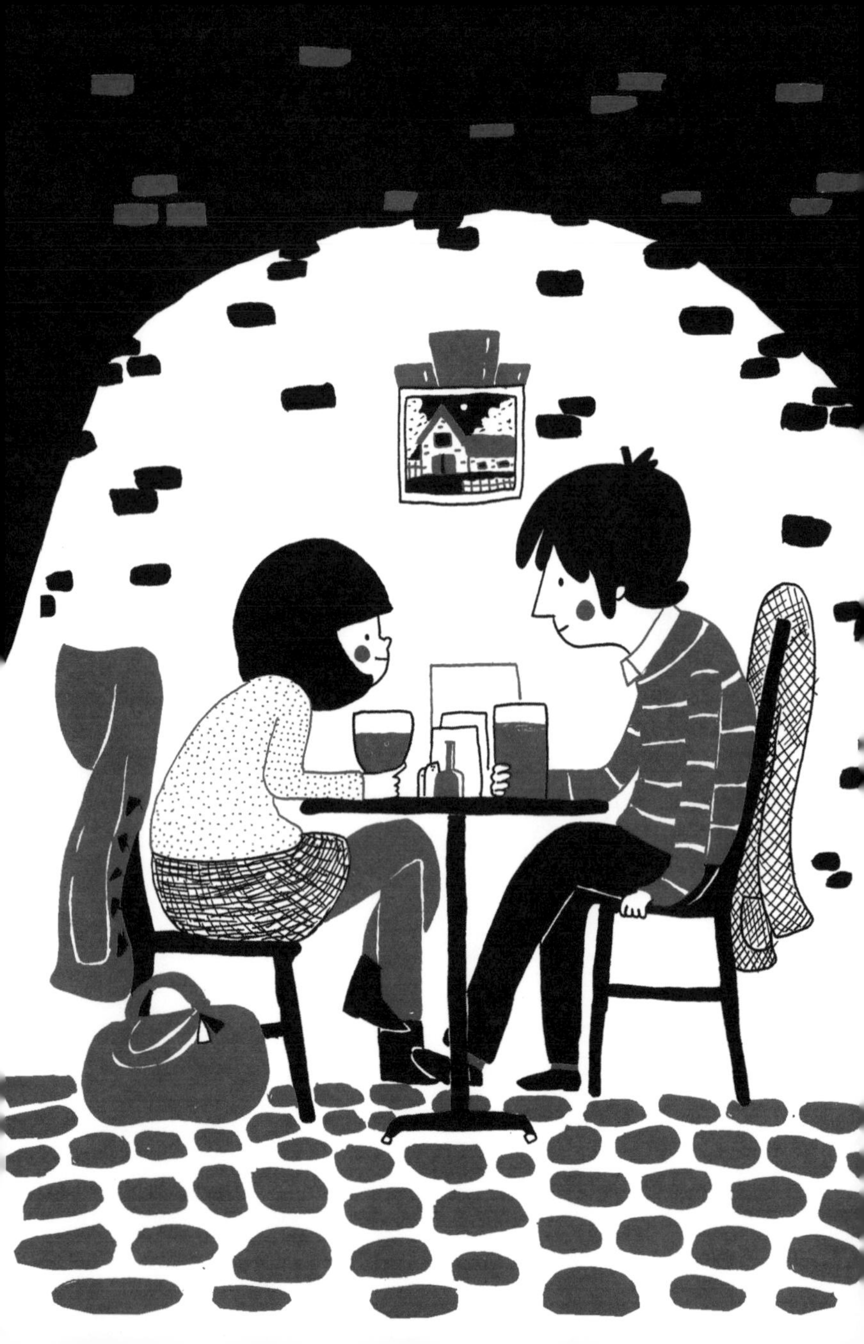

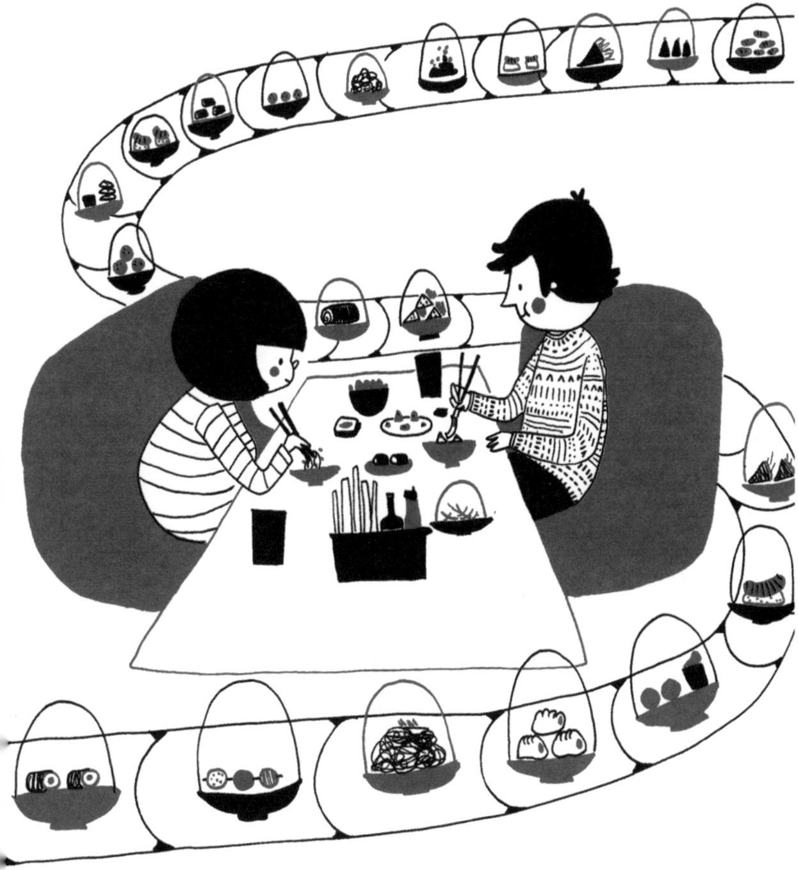

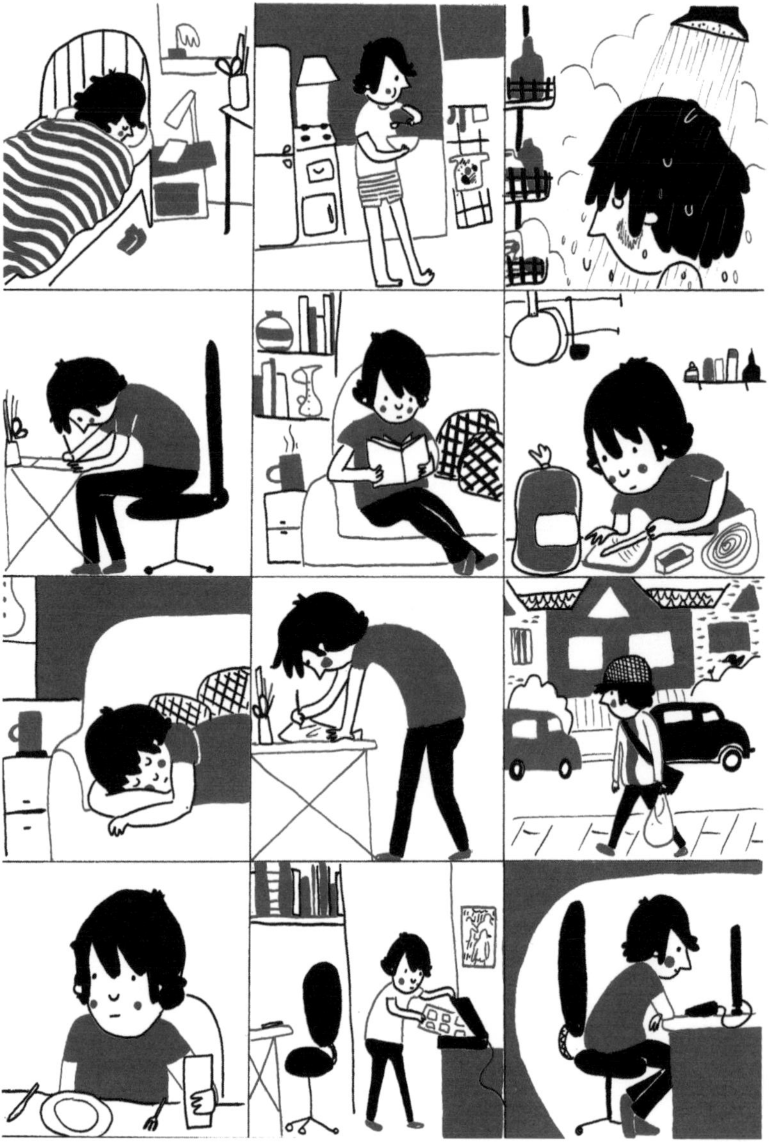

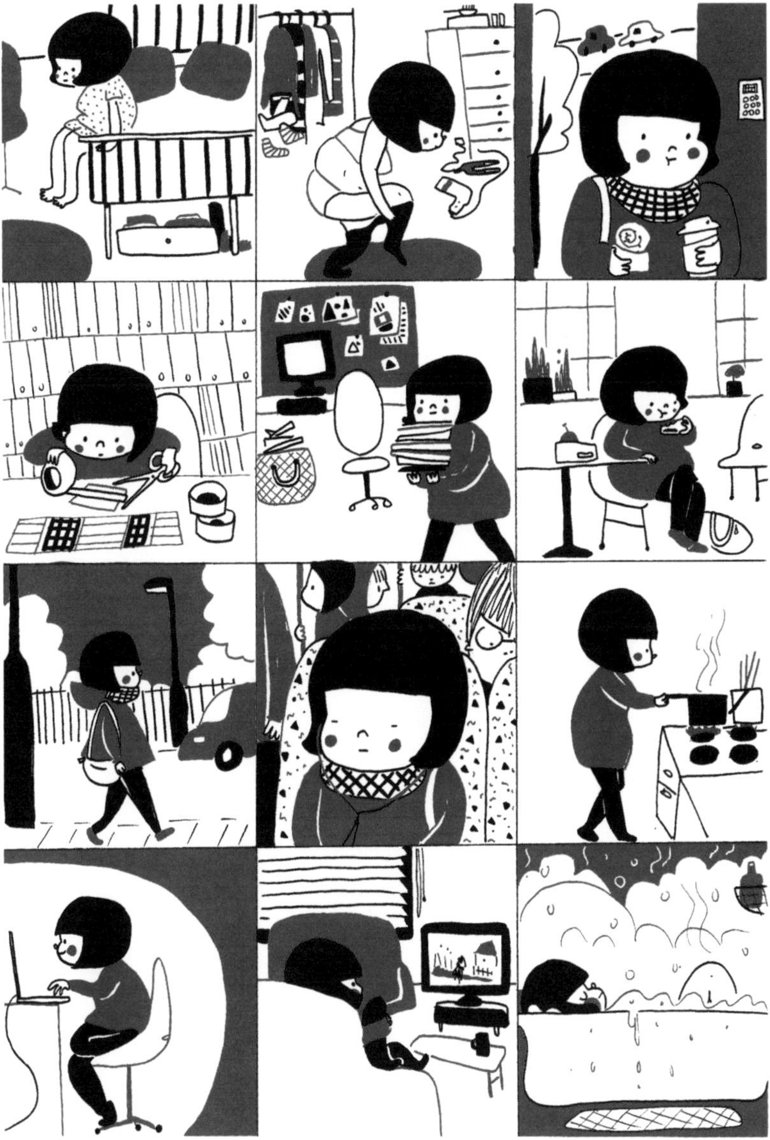

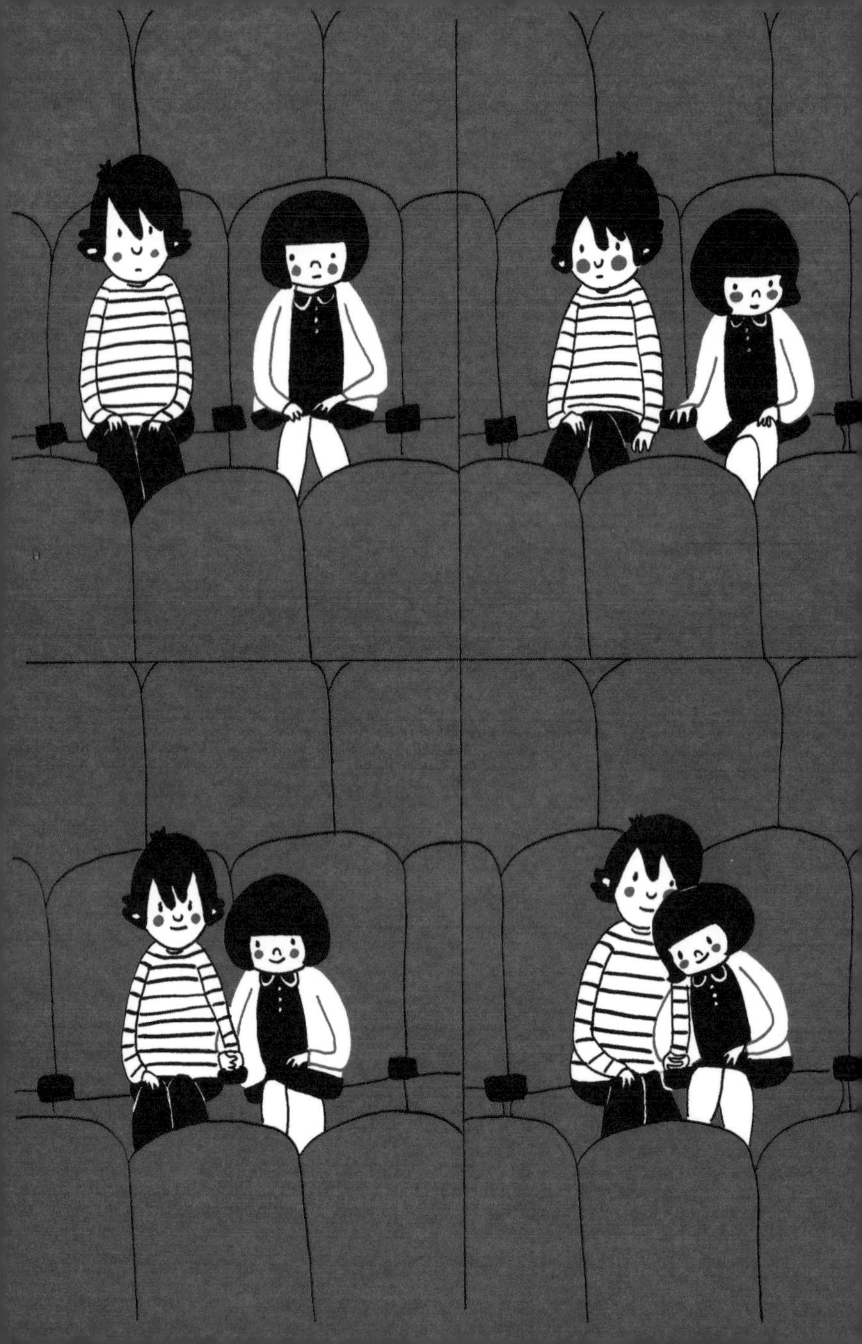

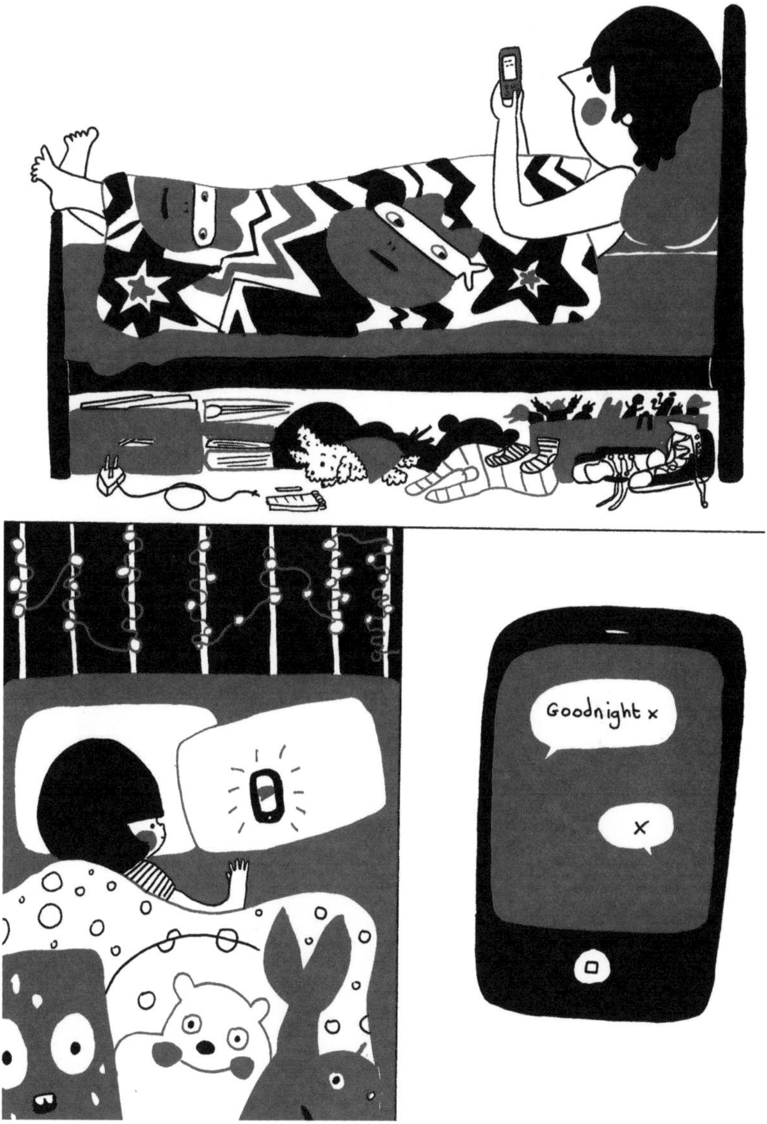
Goodnight x
x

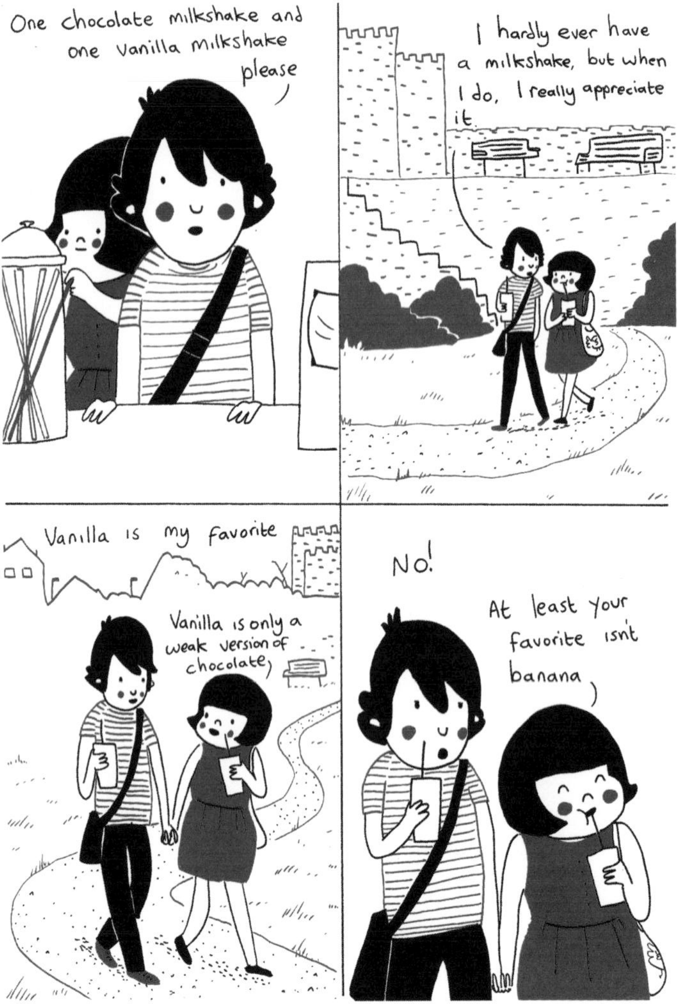
One chocolate milkshake and one vanilla milkshake please
I hardly ever have a milkshake, but when I do, I really appreciate it
Vanilla is my favorite
Vanilla is only a weak version of chocolate
No!
At least your favorite isn't banana

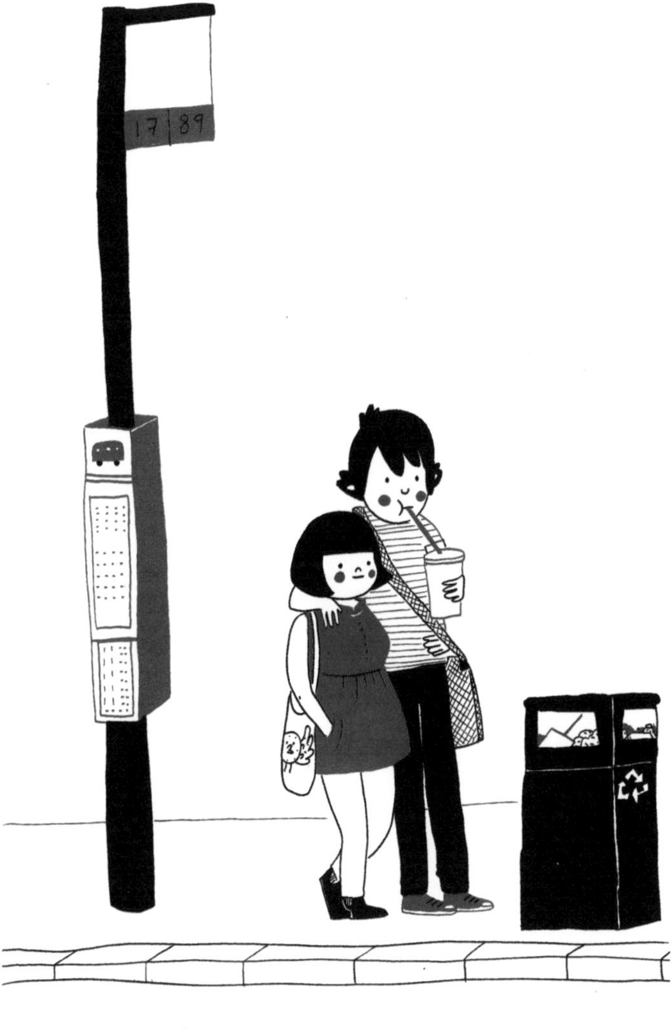
17 | 89

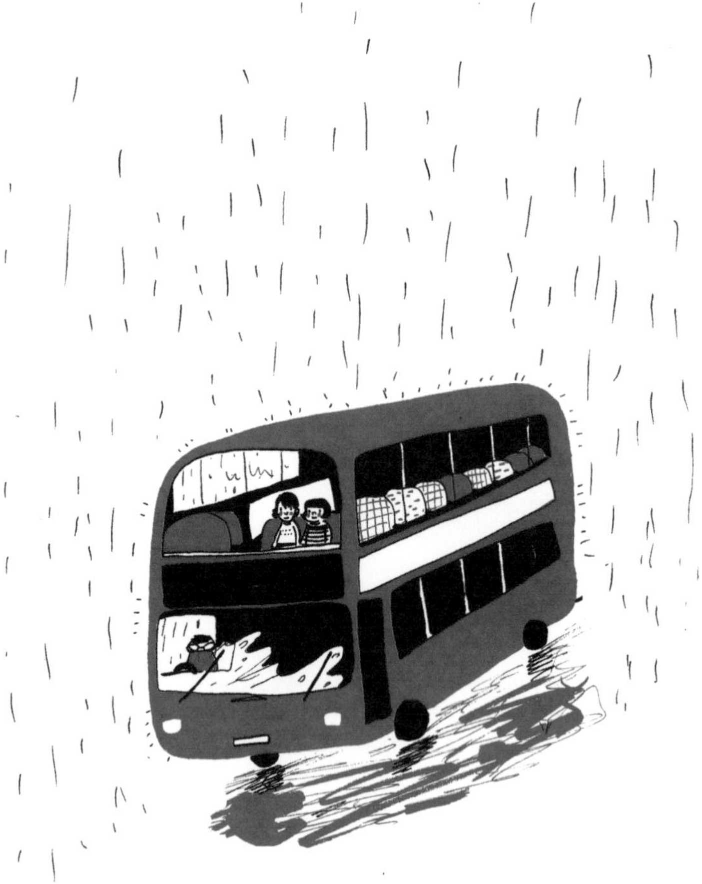

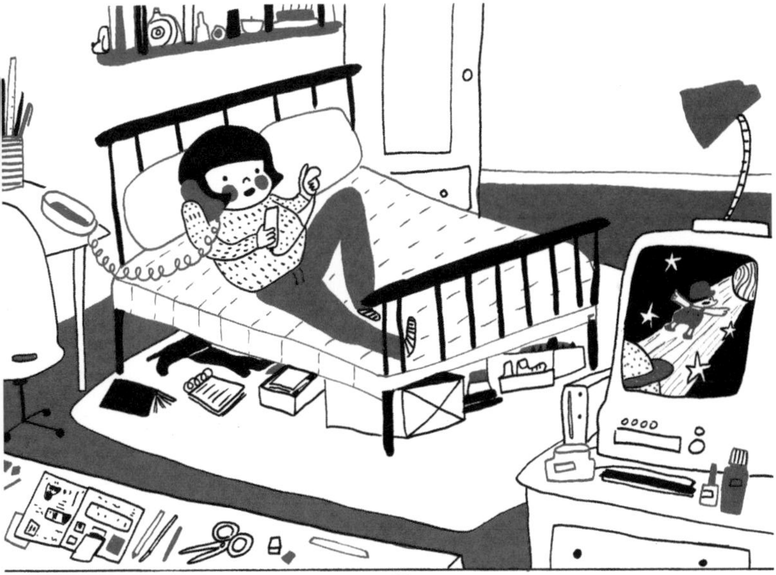

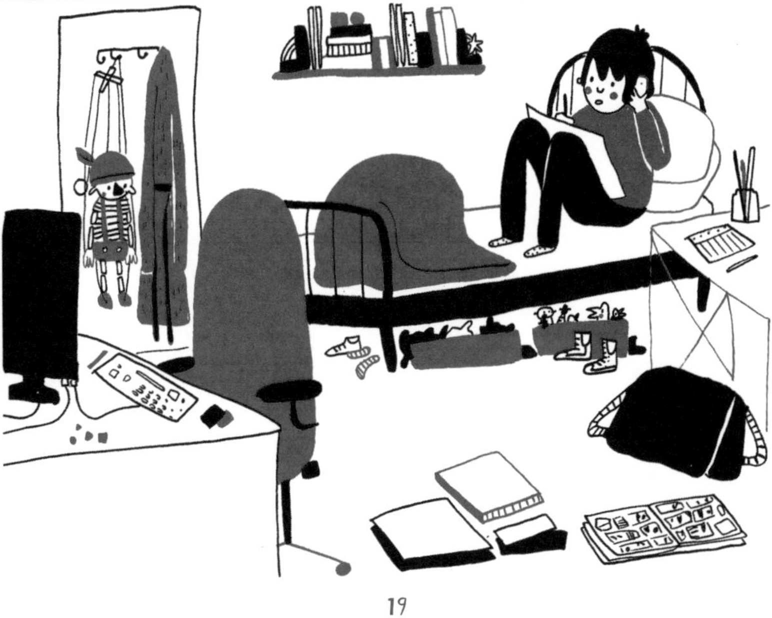

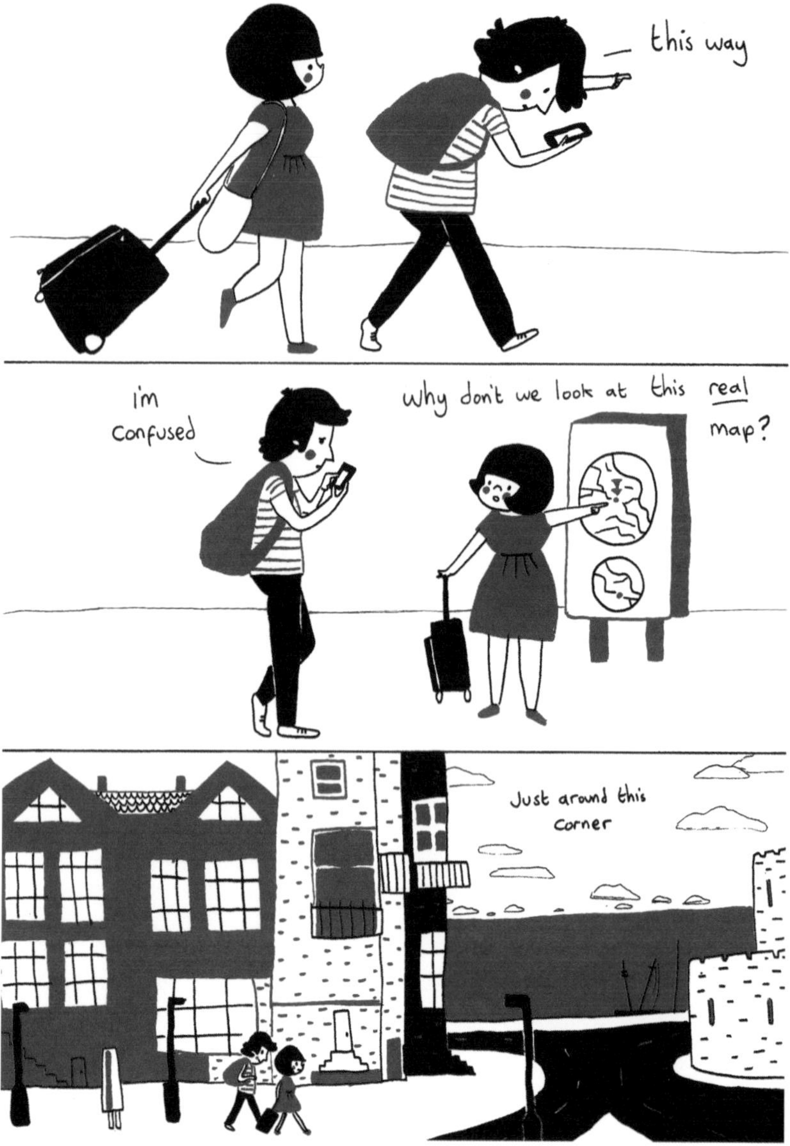
this way
i'm confused
why don't we look at this real map?
Just around this corner

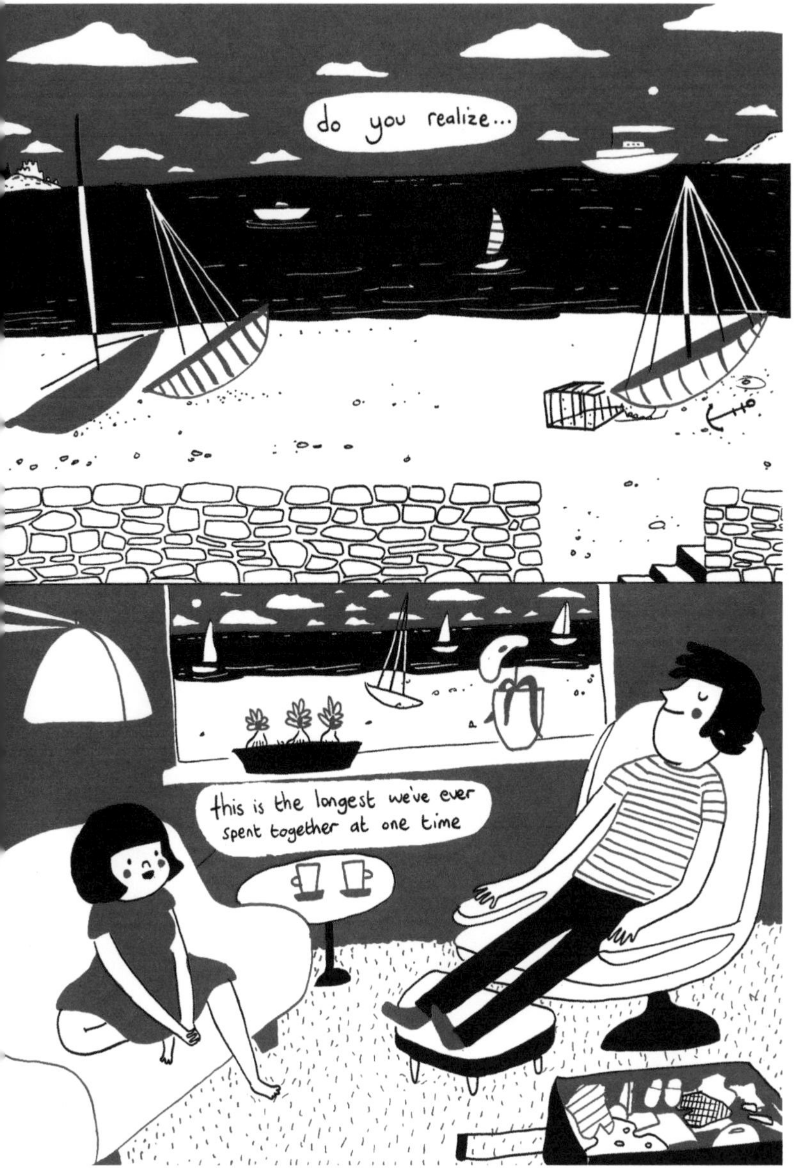
do you realize...
this is the longest we've ever spent together at one time

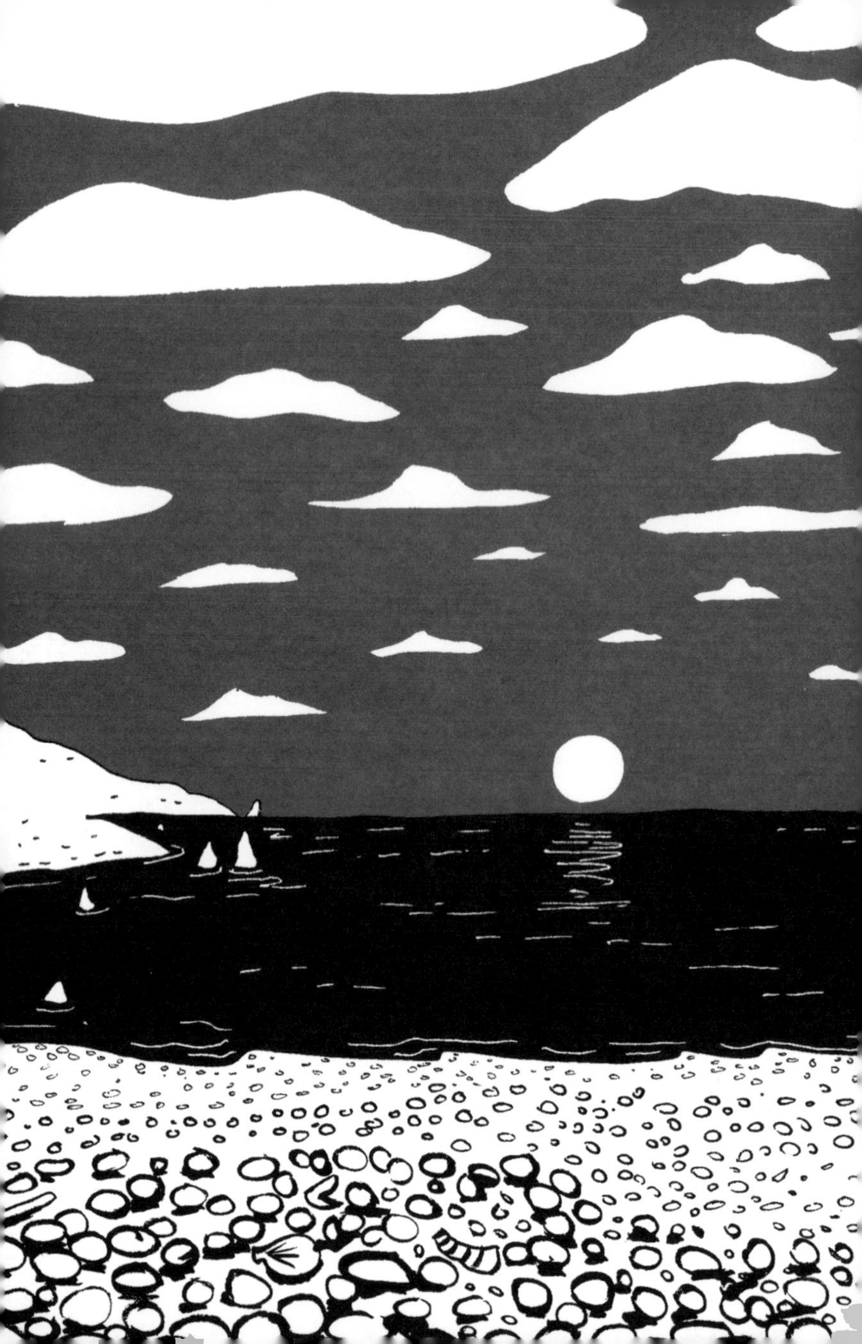

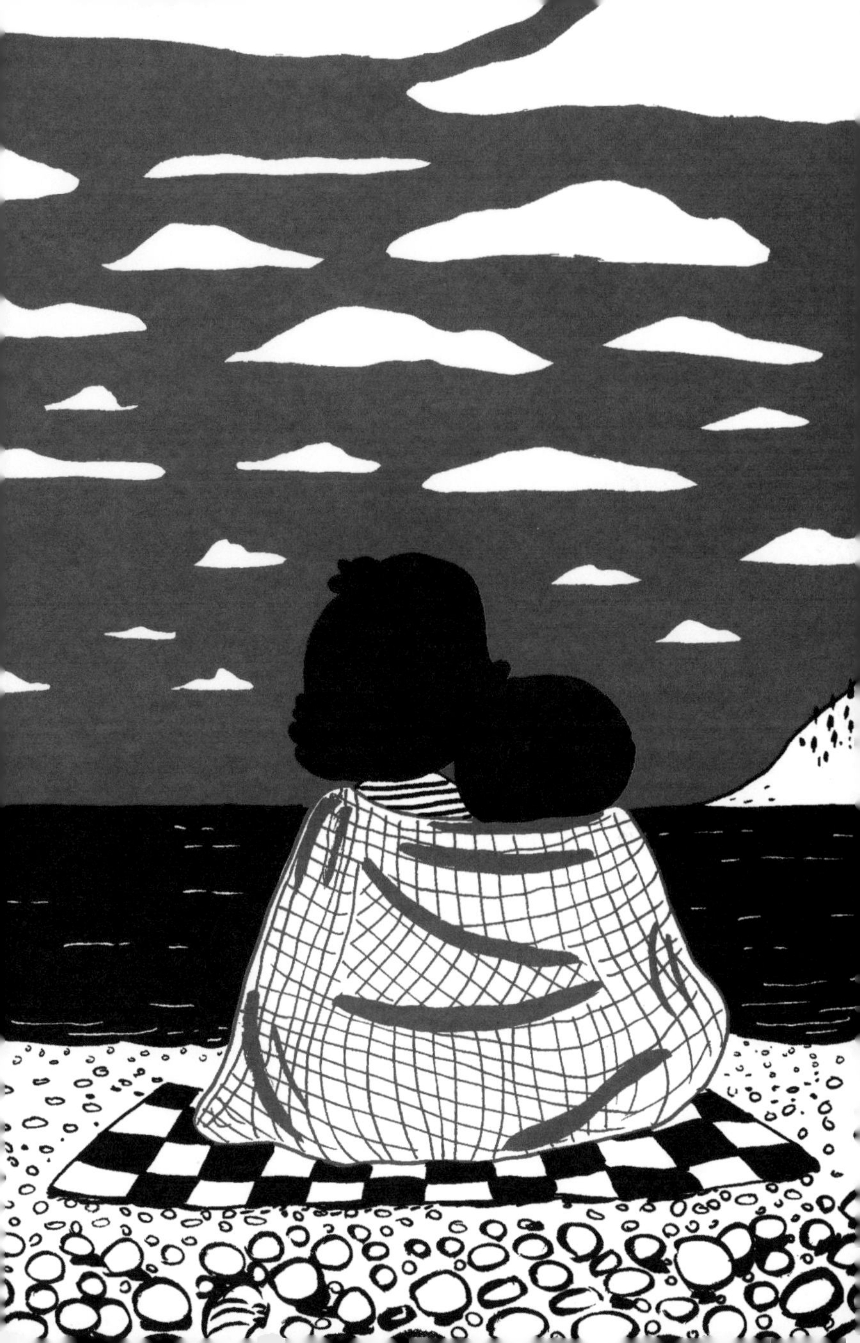

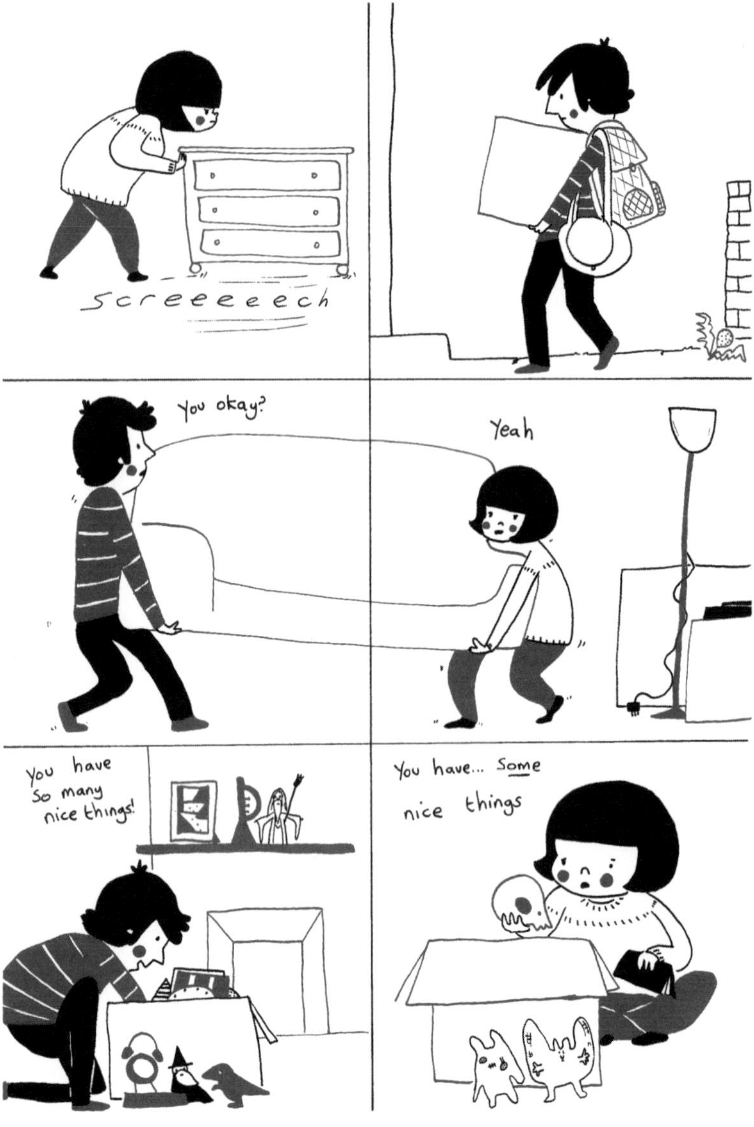
Screeeeeech
You okay?
Yeah
You have so many nice things!
You have... Some nice things

25

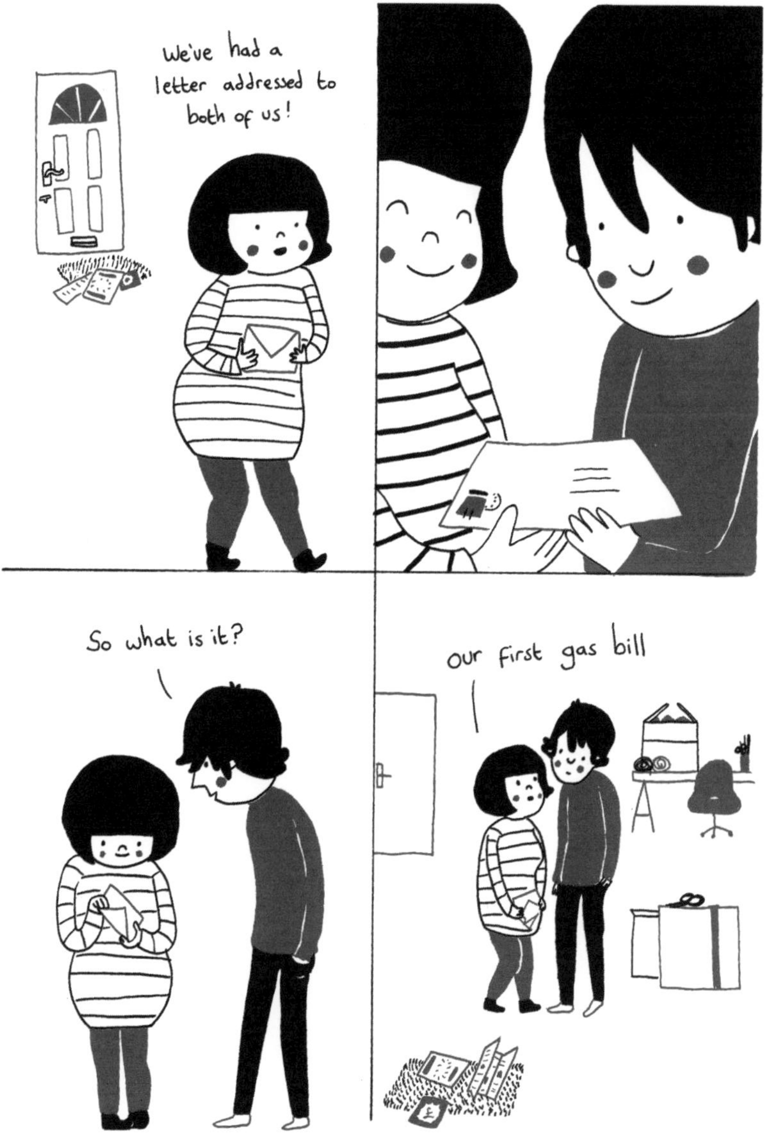
We've had a letter addressed to both of us!
So what is it?
our first gas bill

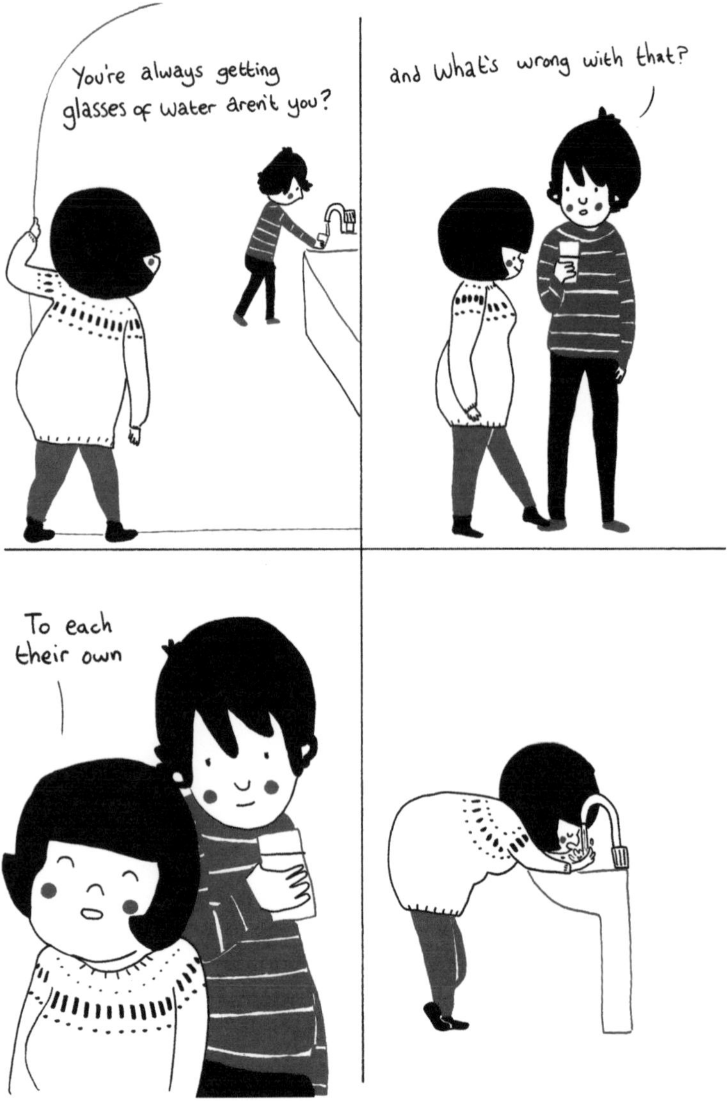
You're always getting glasses of water aren't you?
and what's wrong with that?
To each their own

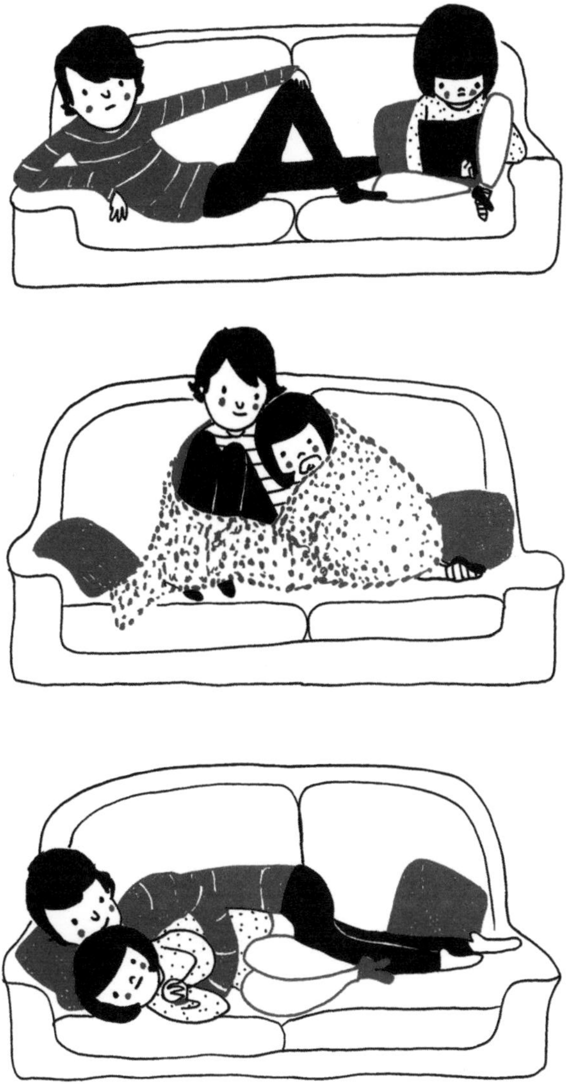

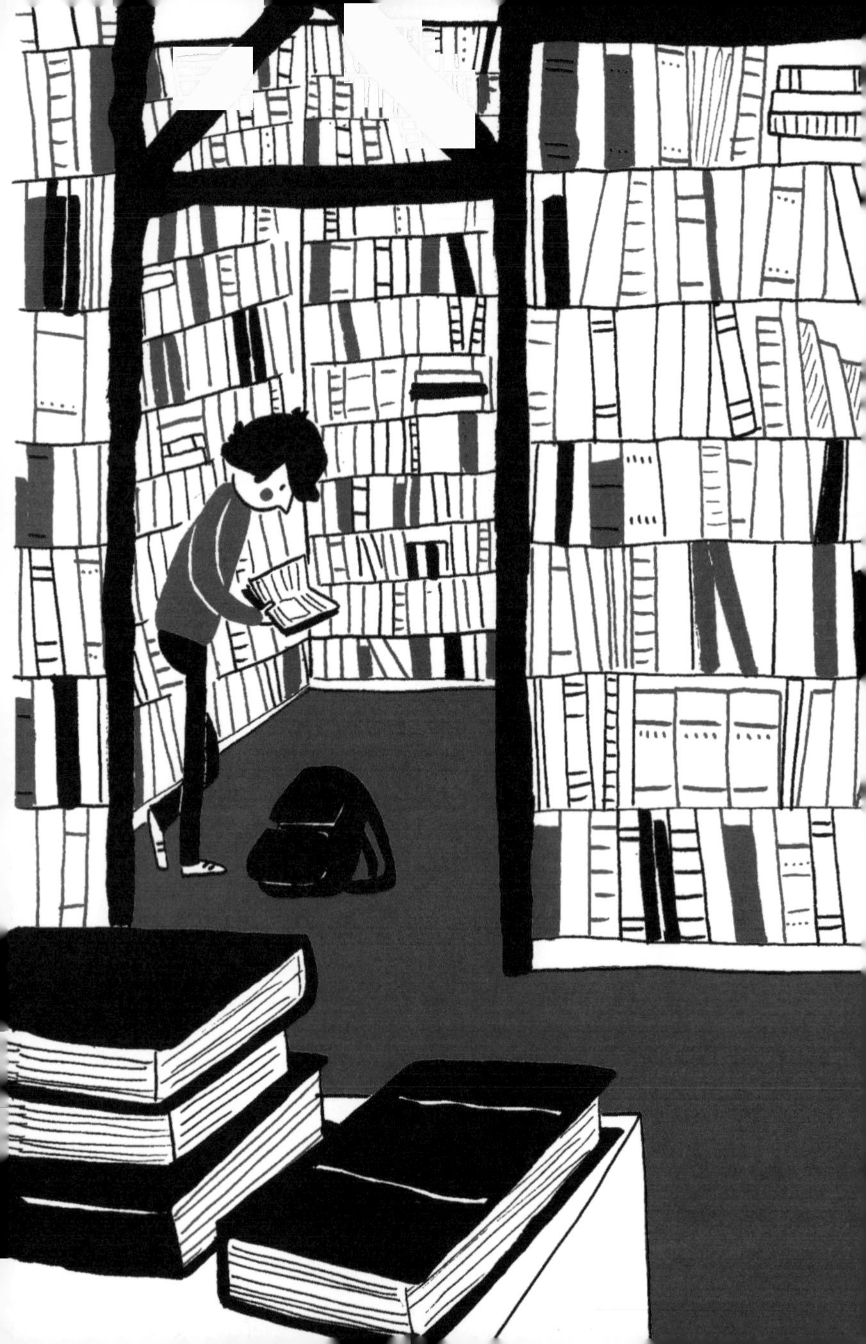

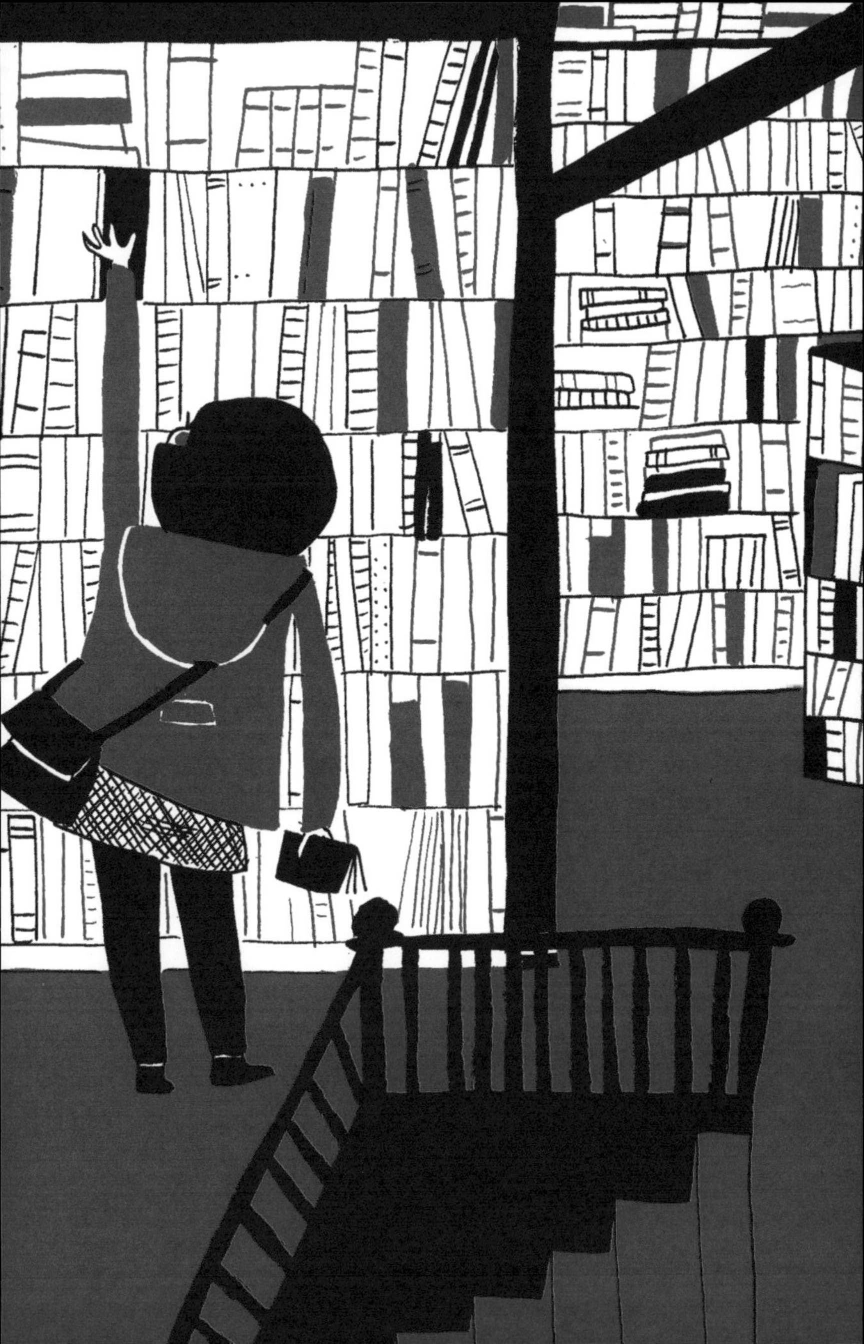

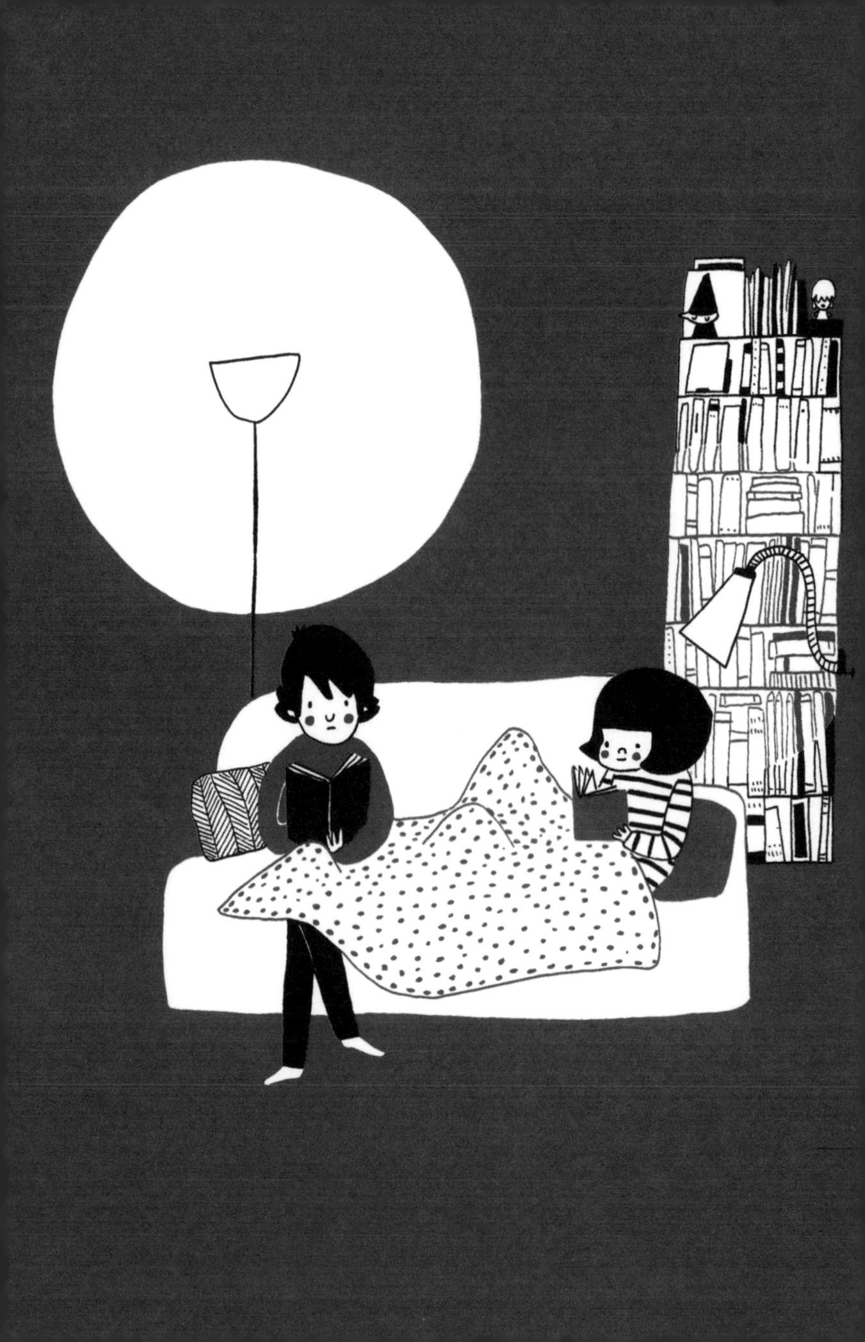

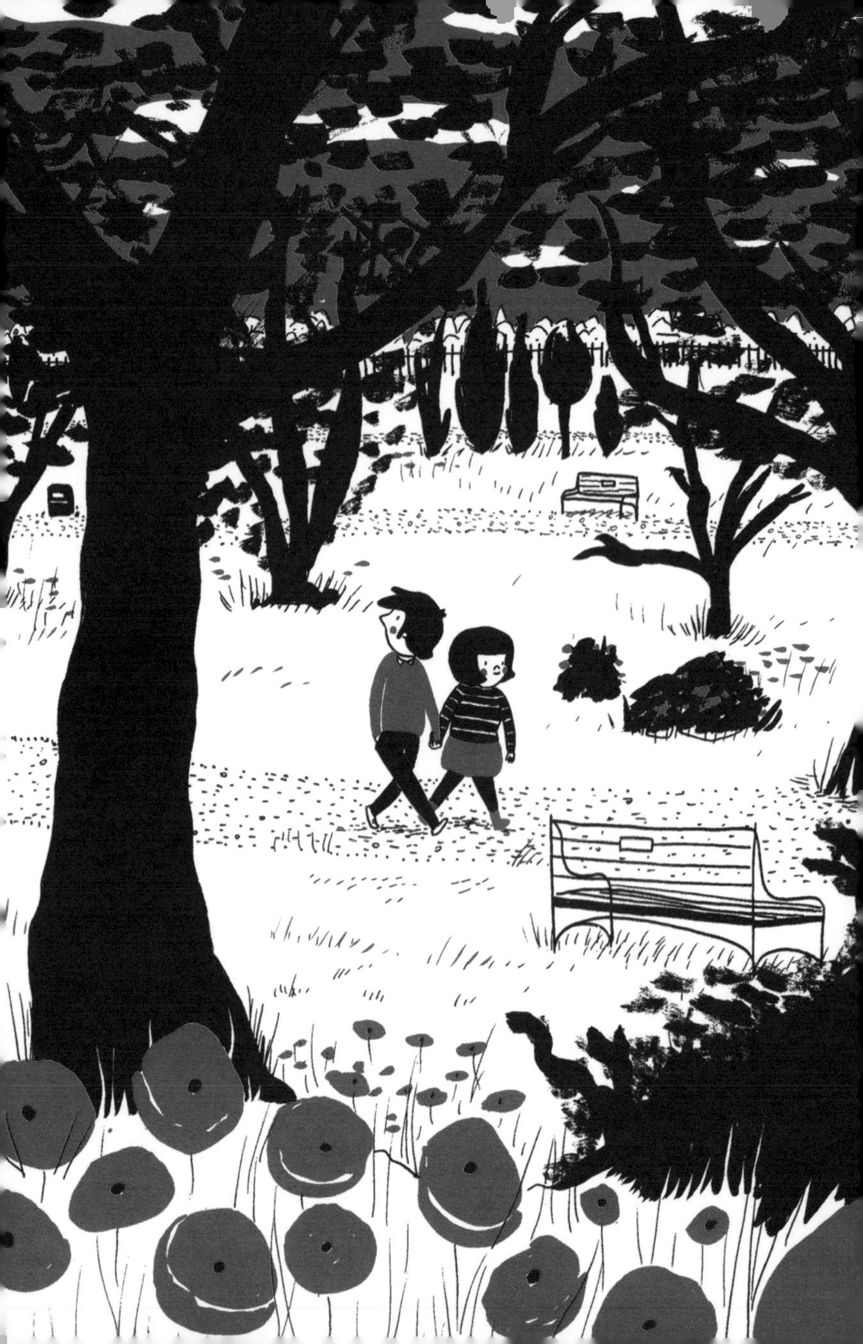

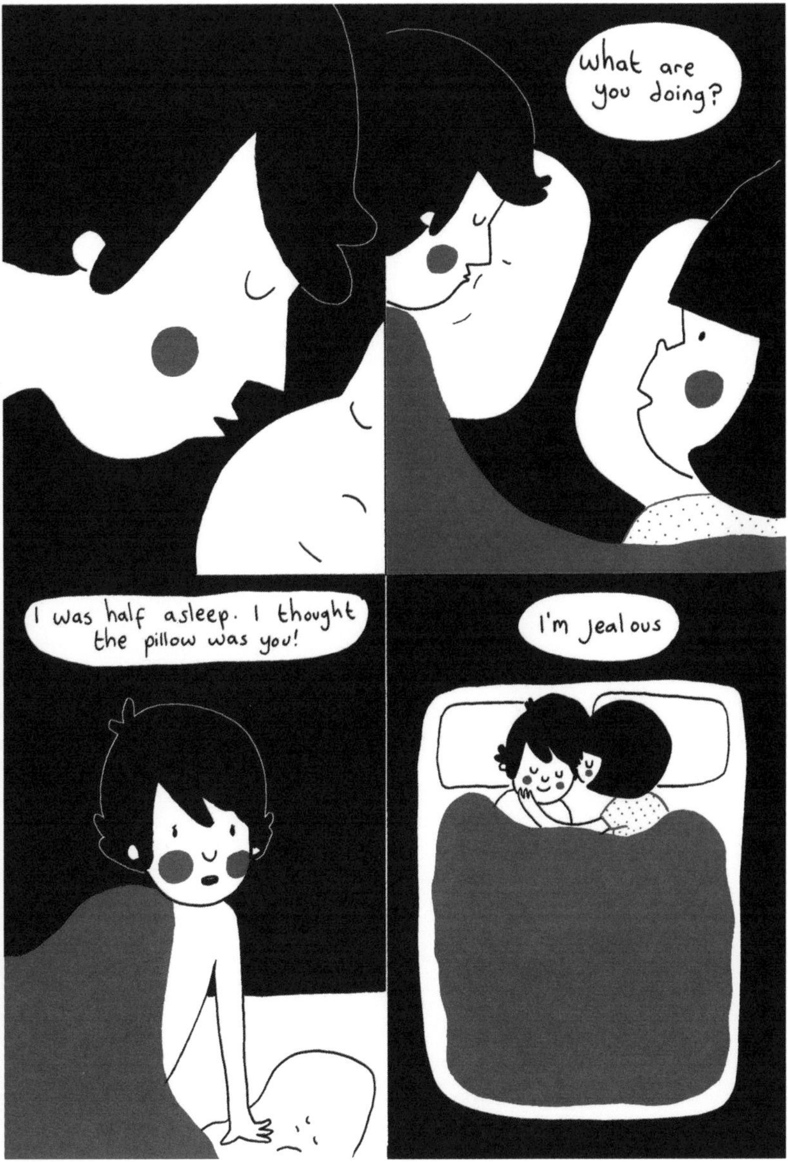
what are you doing?
I was half asleep. I thought the pillow was you!
I'm jealous

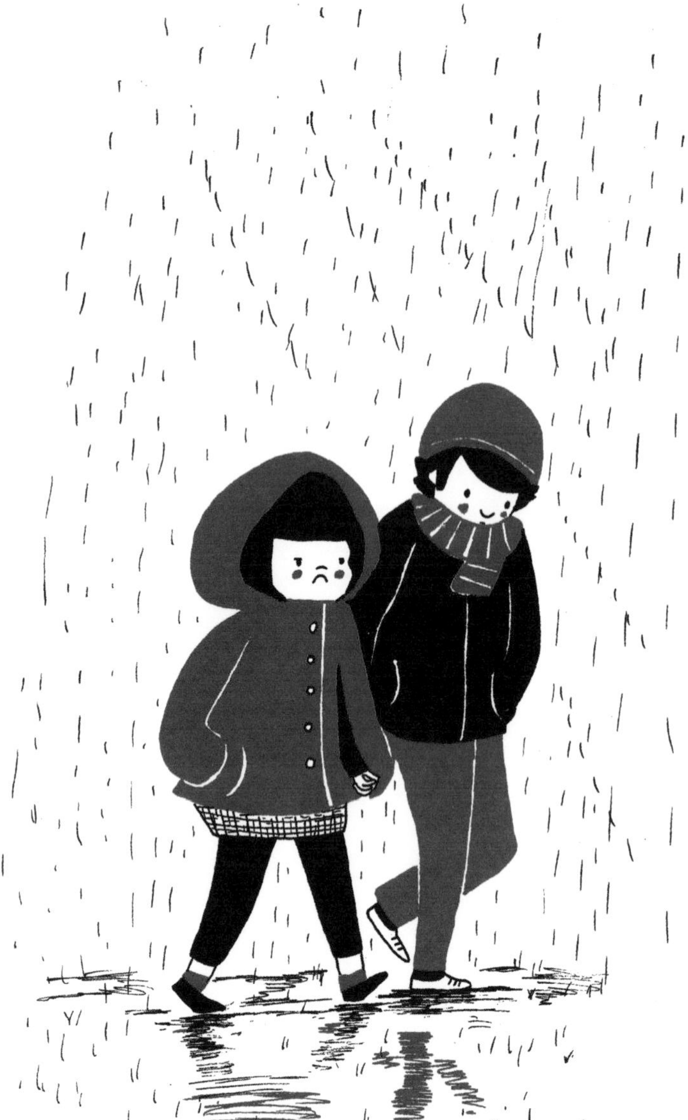

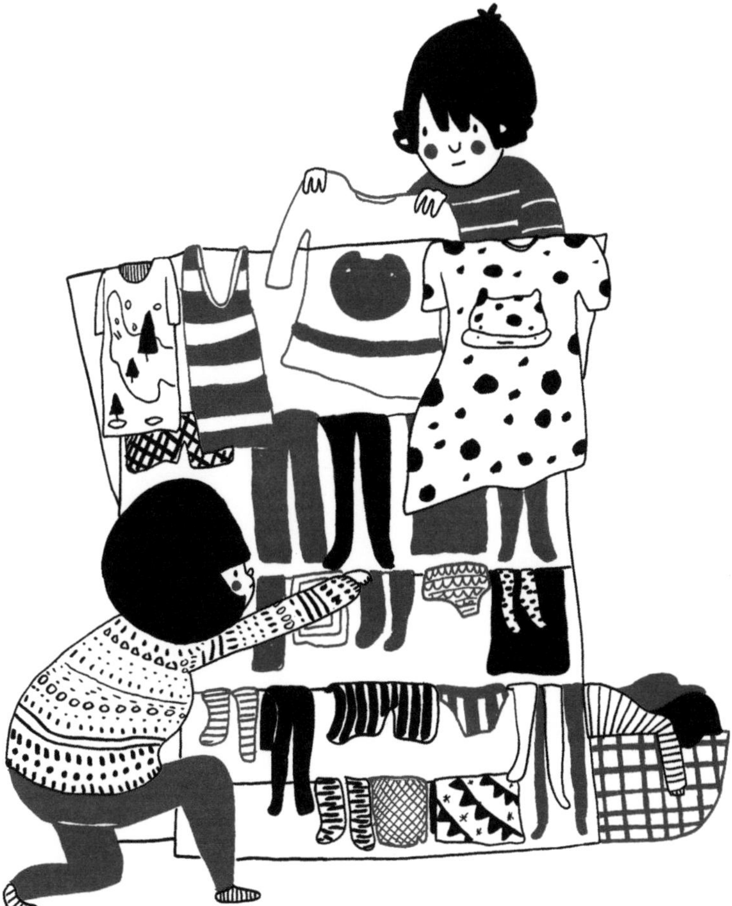

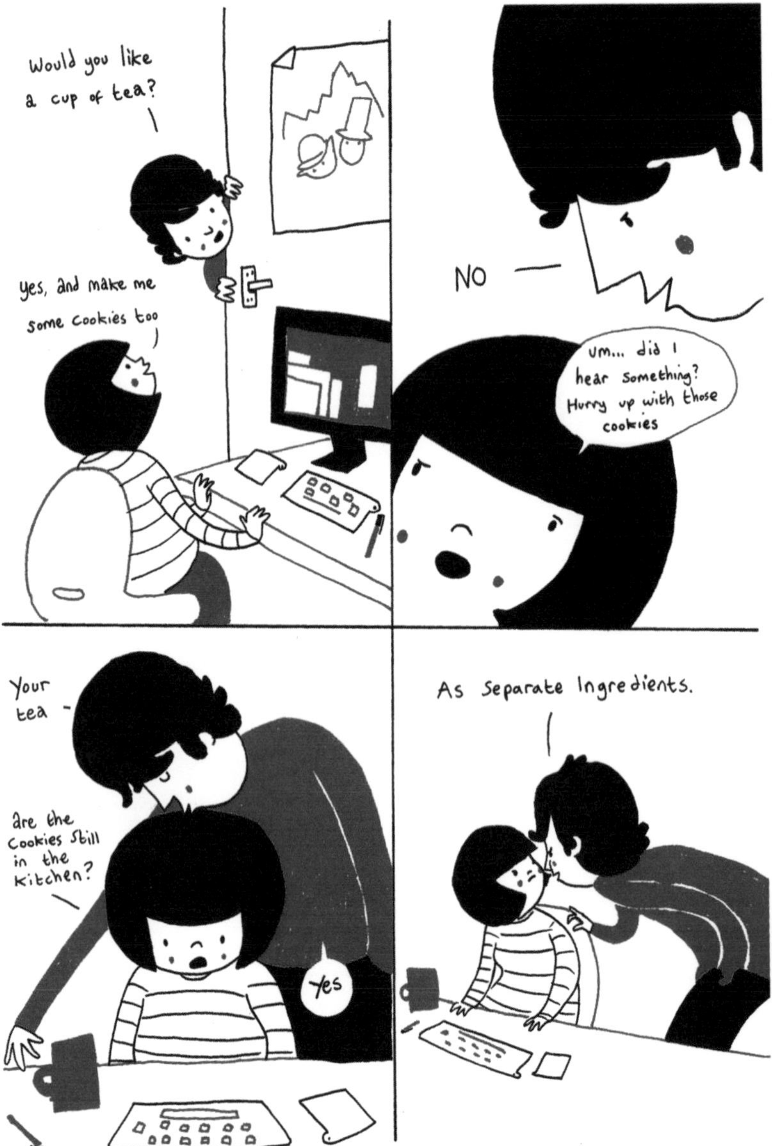
Would you like a cup of tea?
yes, and make me some cookies too
NO
um... did I hear something? Hurry up with those cookies
Your tea
are the cookies still in the kitchen?
yes
As Separate Ingredients.

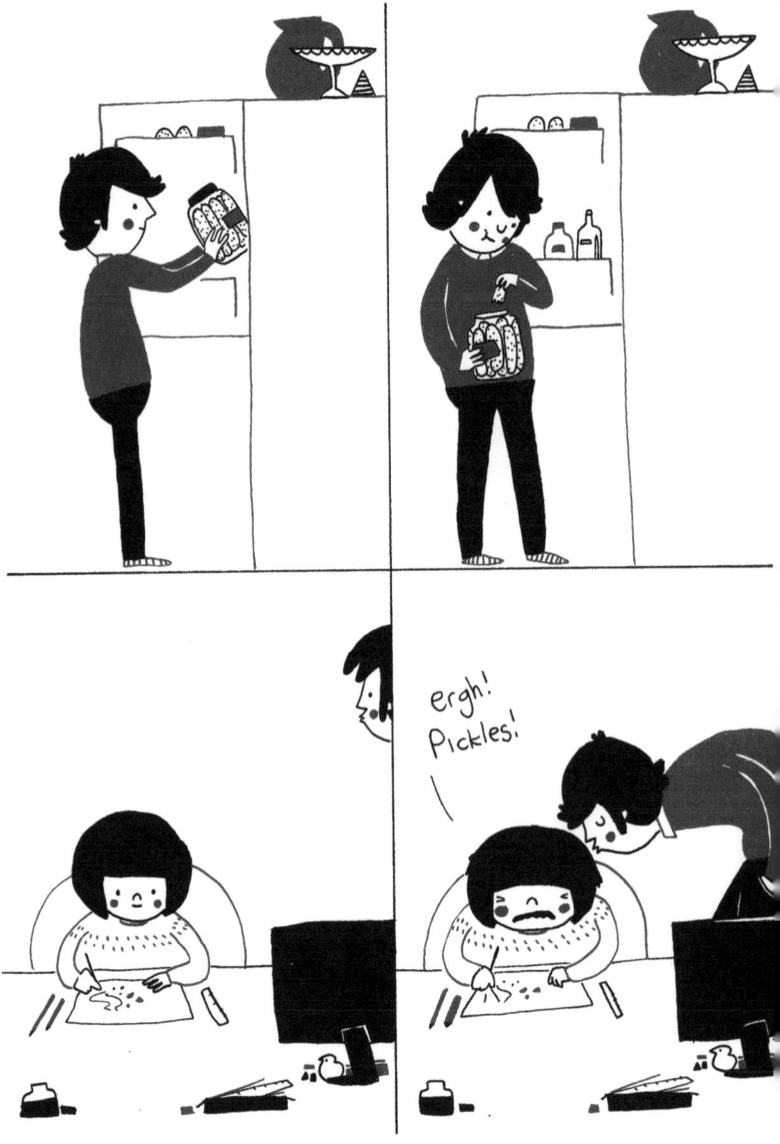
ergh!
Pickles!

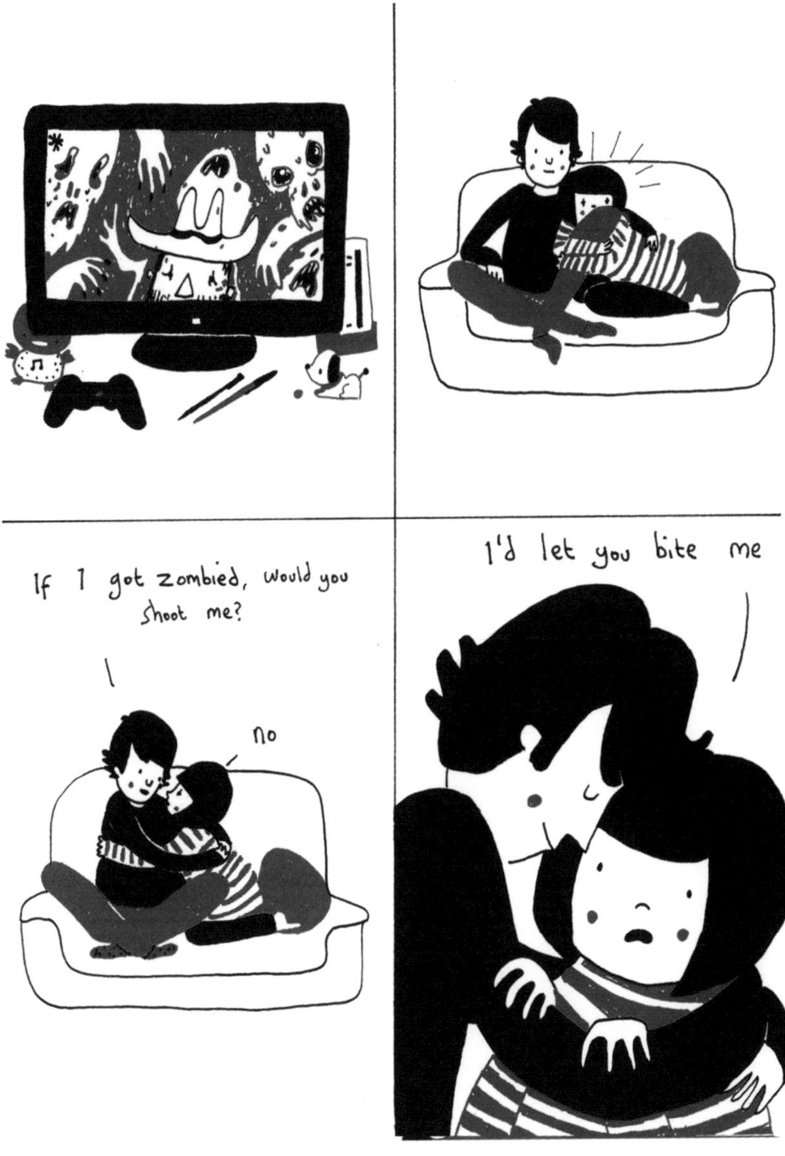
If I got zombied, would you shoot me?
no
I'd let you bite me

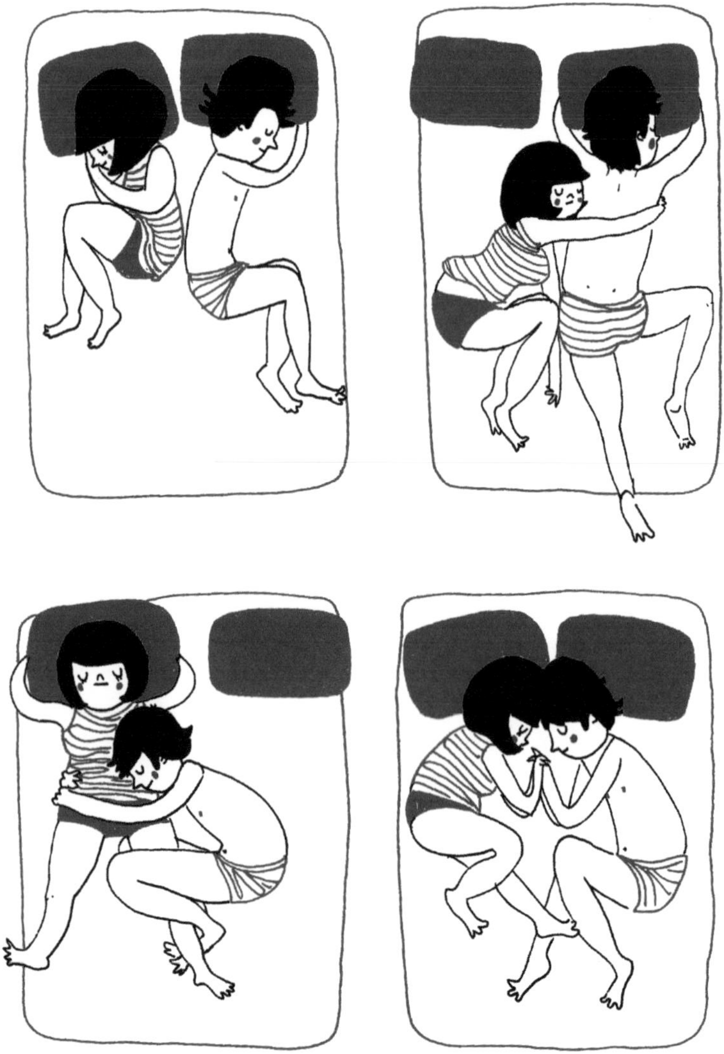

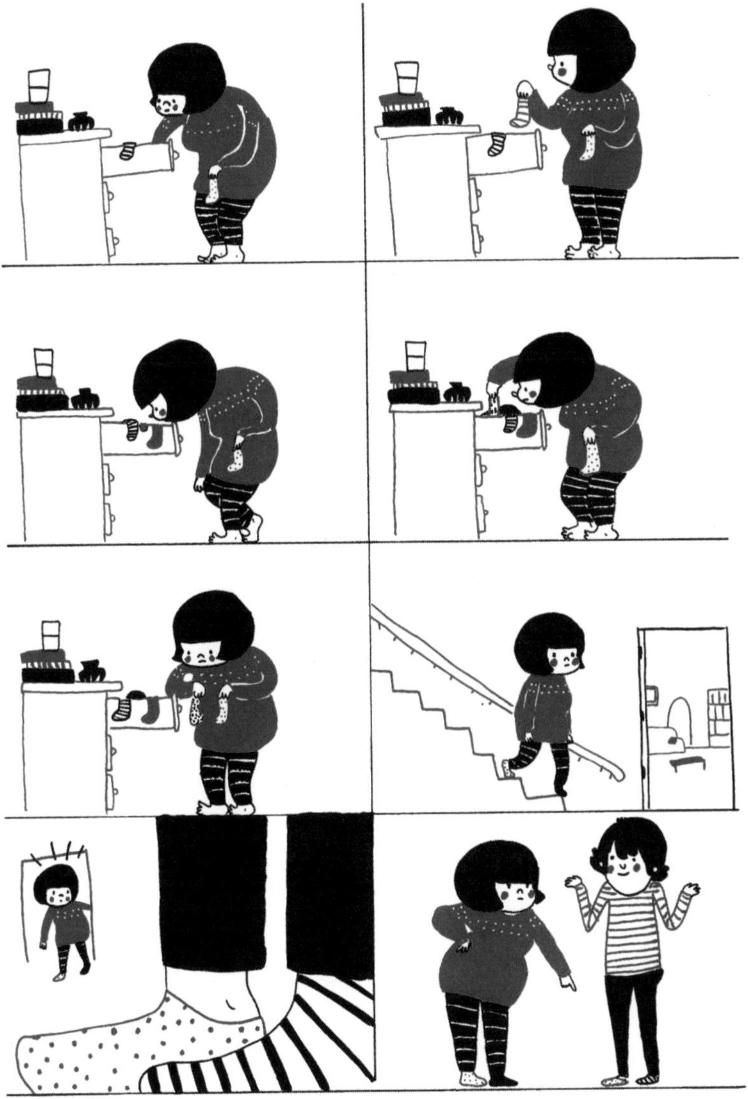

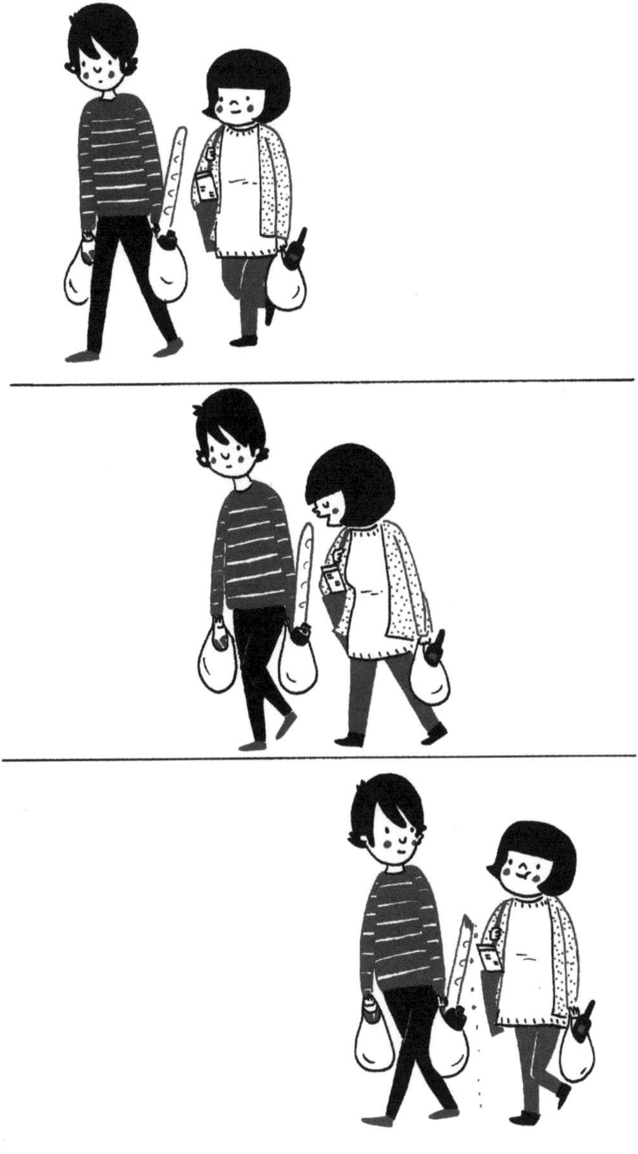

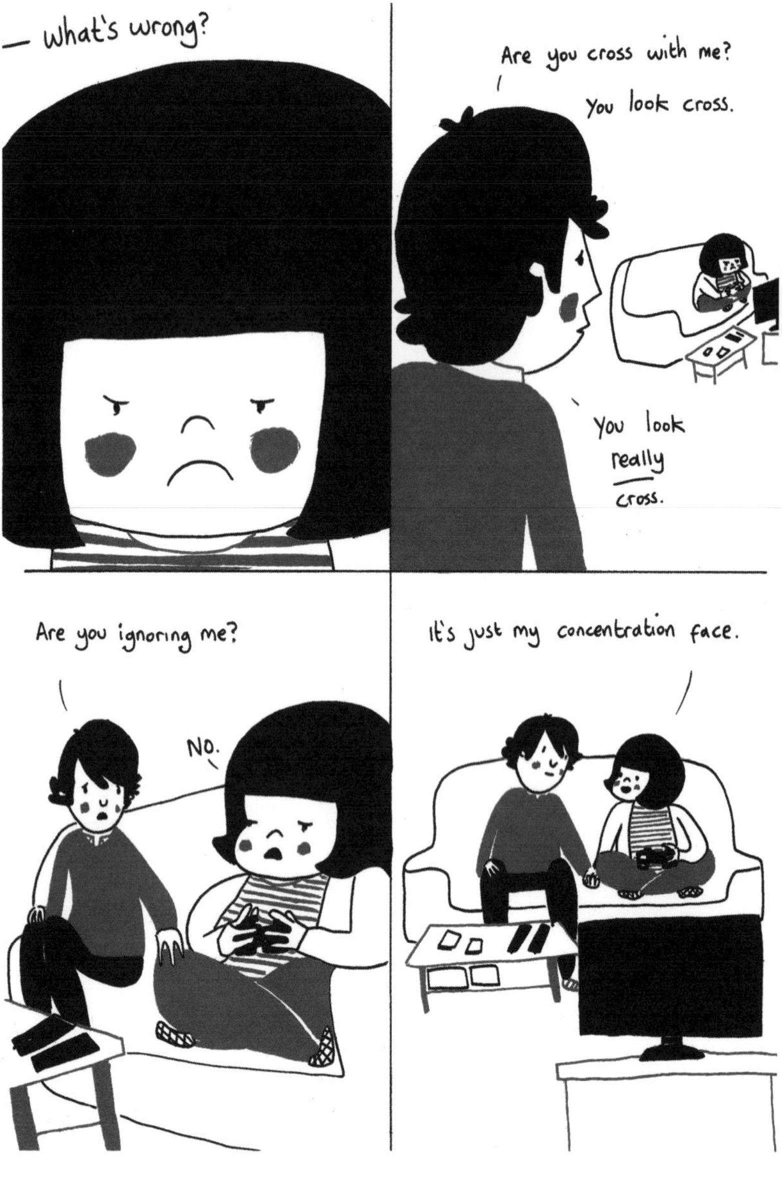
— What's wrong?
Are you cross with me?
You look cross.
You look really cross.
Are you ignoring me?
No.
It's just my concentration face.

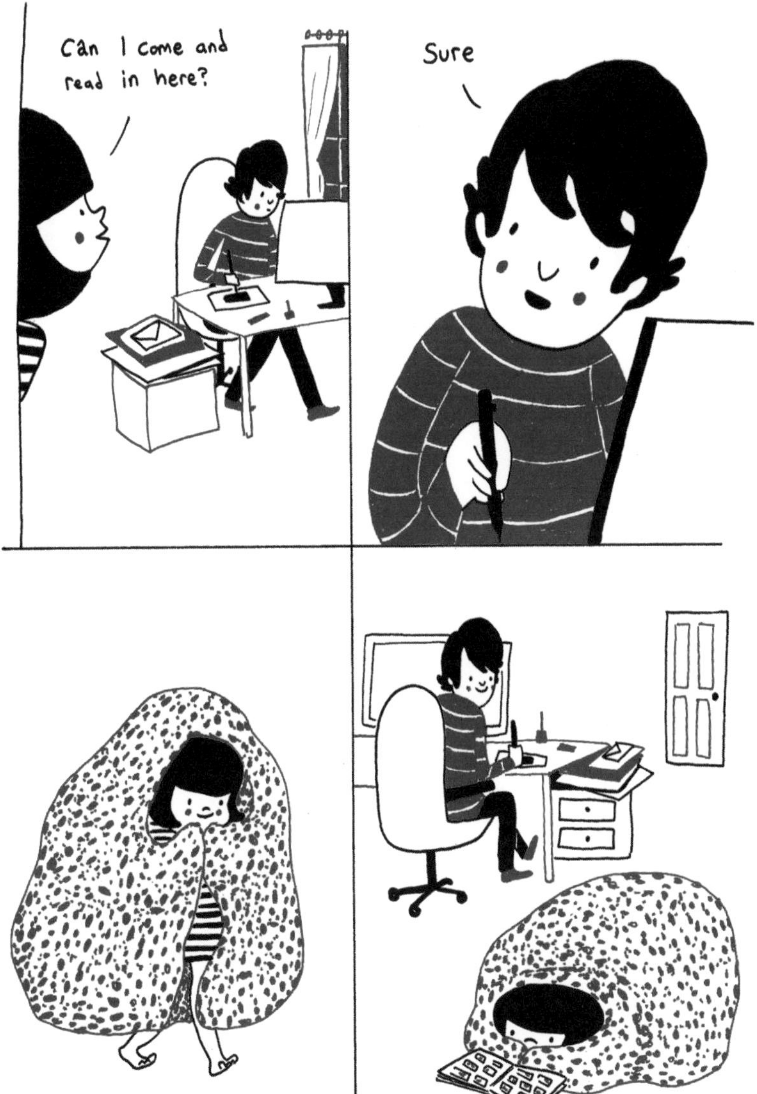
Can I come and read in here?
Sure

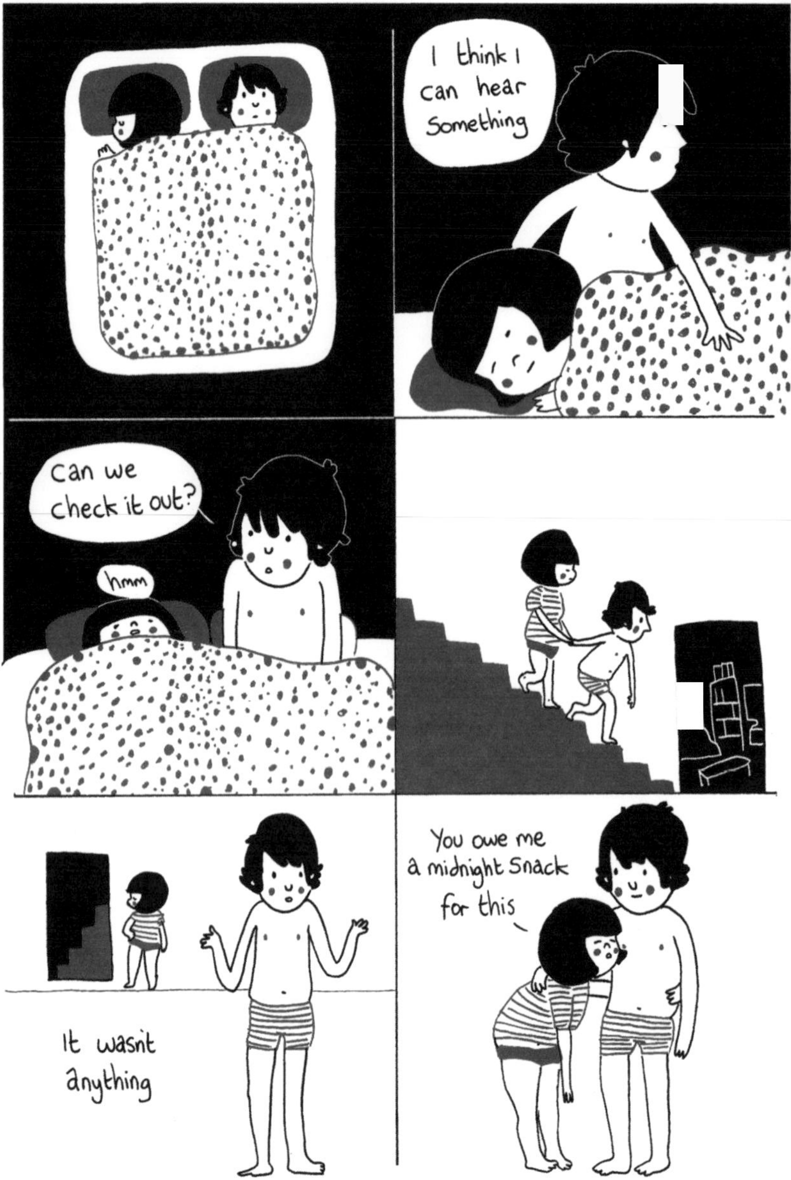
I think I can hear Something
Can we check it out?
hmm
It wasn't anything
You owe me a midnight Snack for this

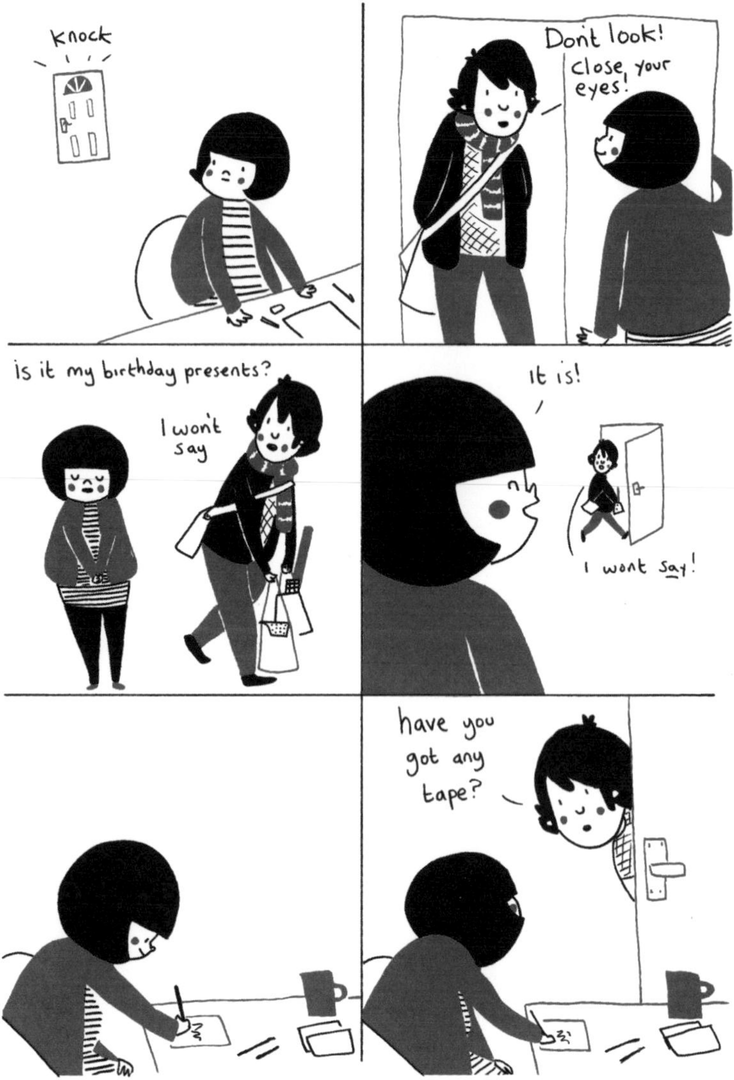
knock
Dont look!
close your eyes!
is it my birthday presents?
I won't say
It is!
I wont say!
have you got any tape?

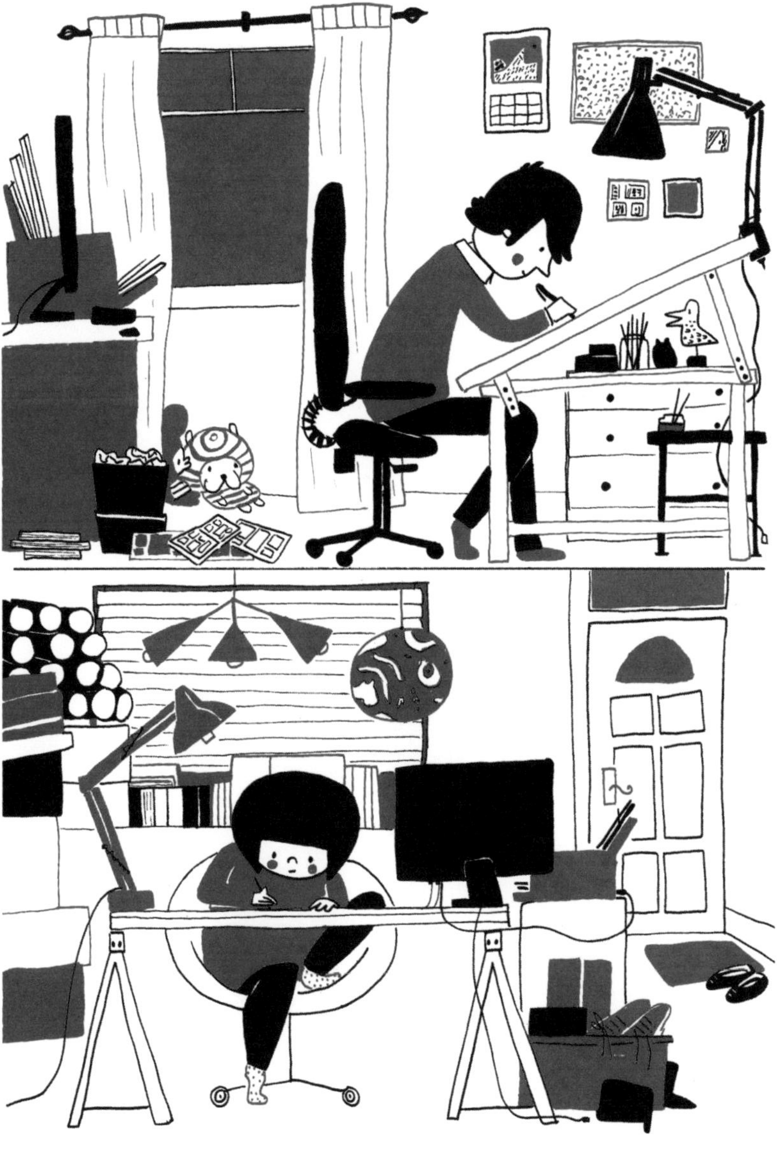

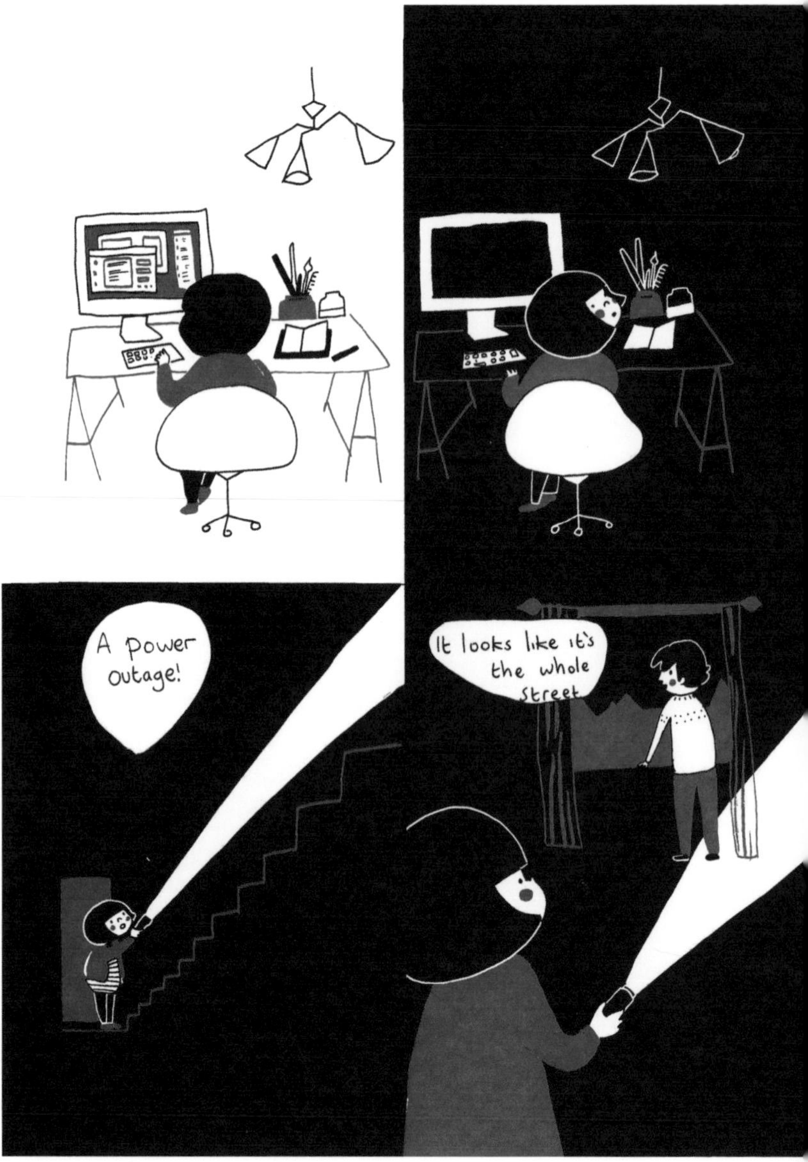
A power outage!
It looks like it's the whole street

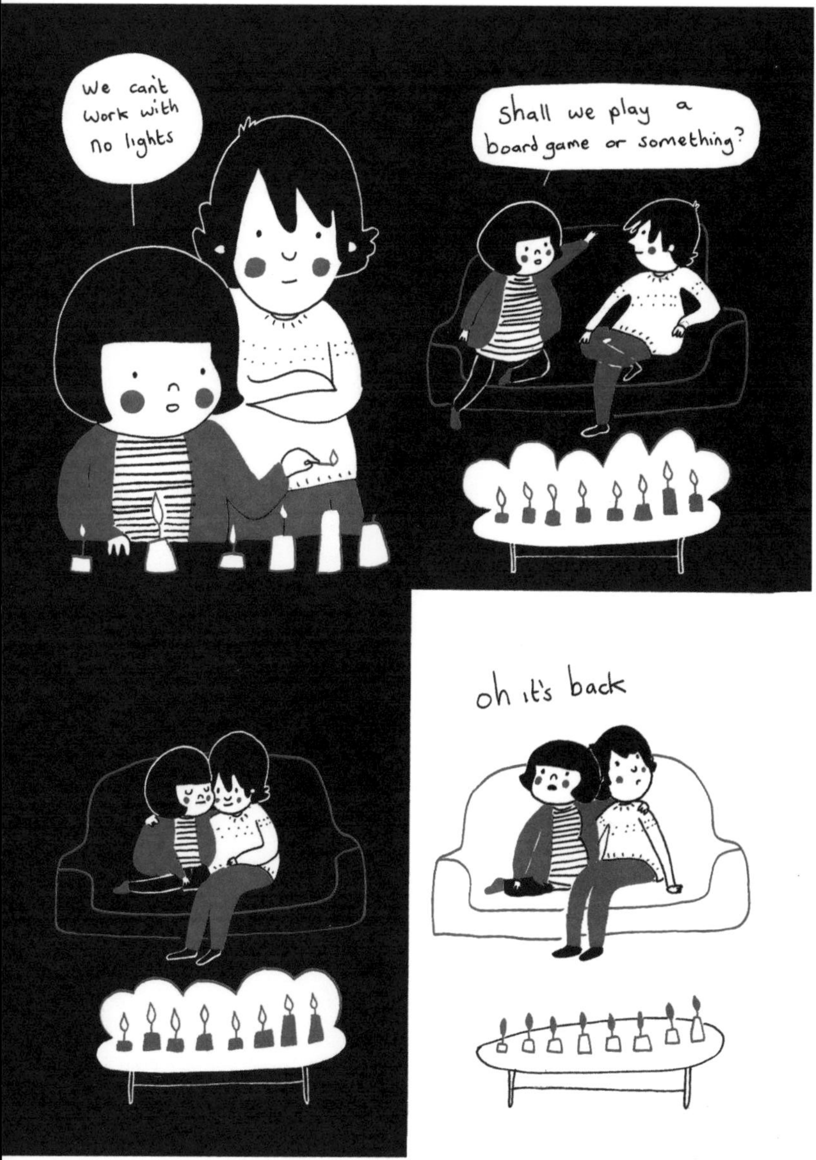
We can't work with no lights
Shall we play a board game or something?
oh it's back

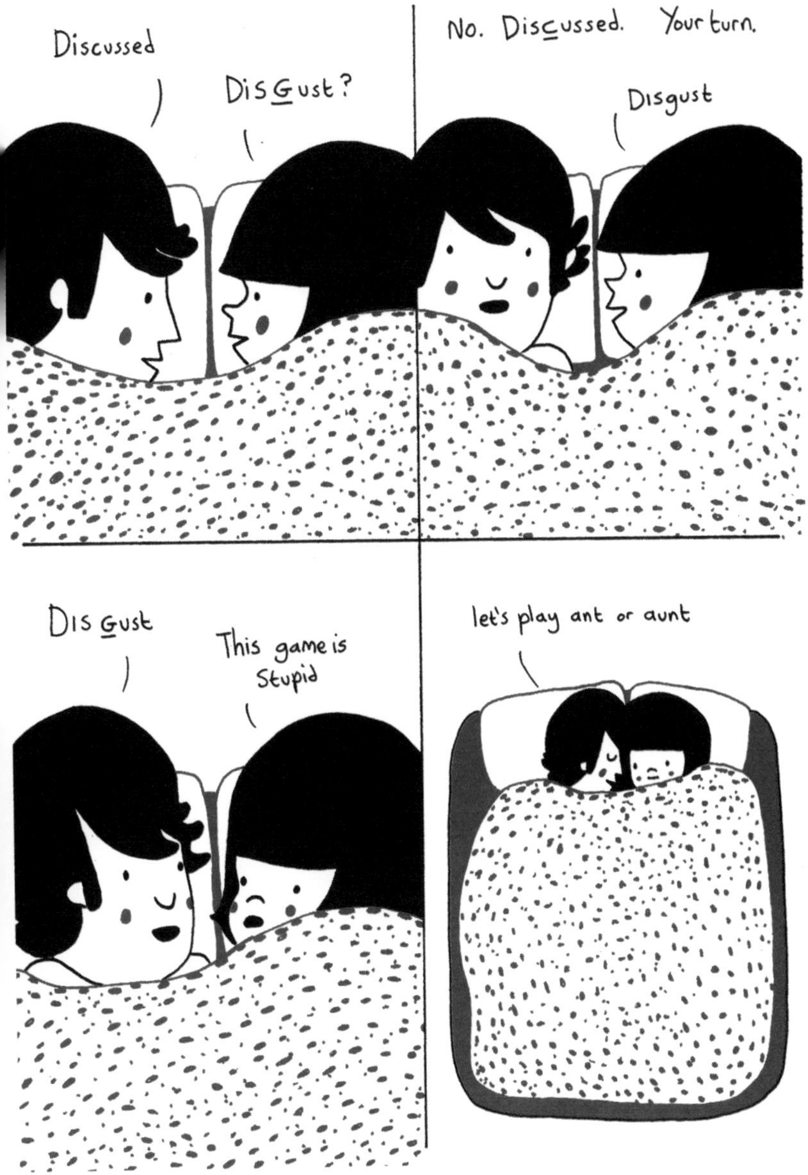
Discussed
DisGust?
No. Discussed. Your turn.
Disgust
DisGust
This game is stupid
let's play ant or aunt

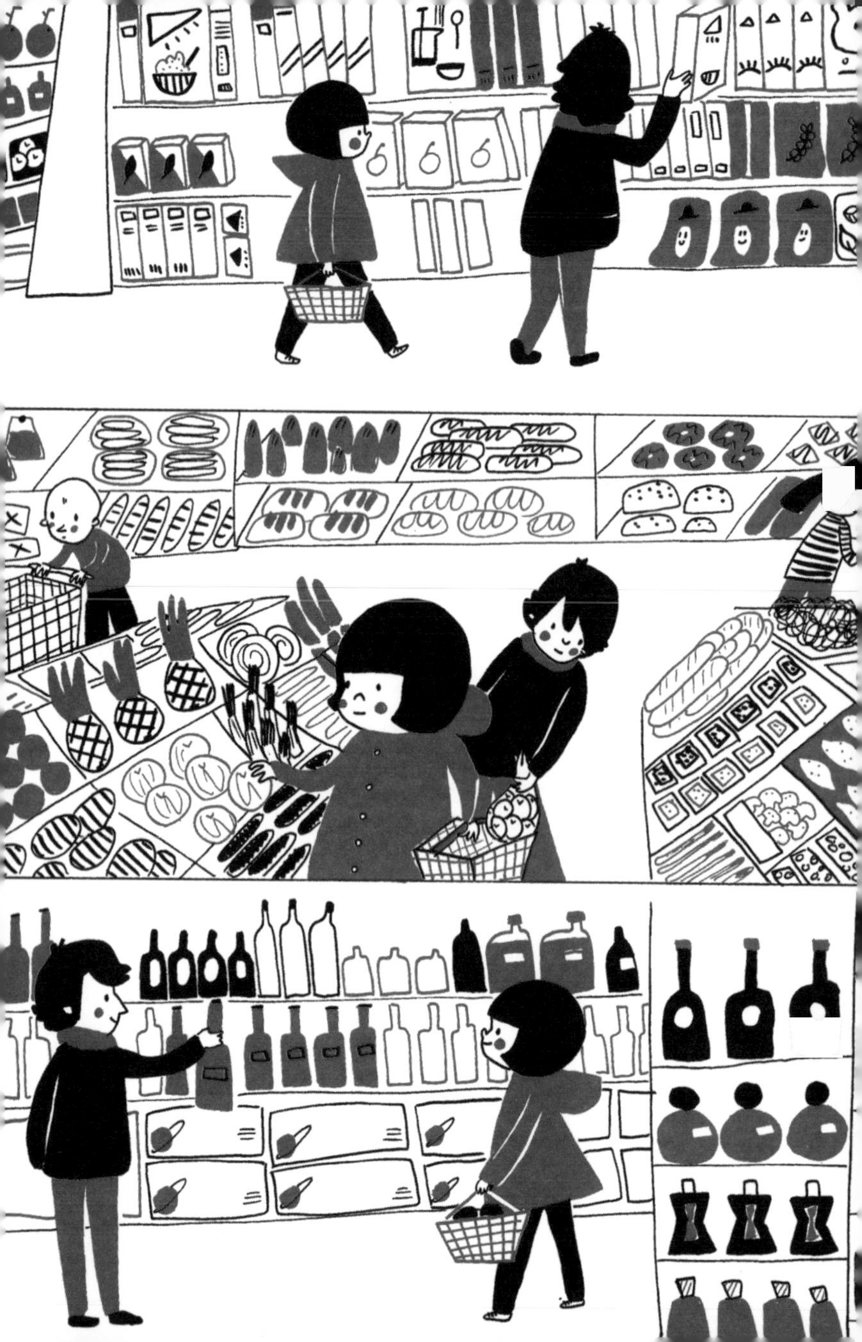

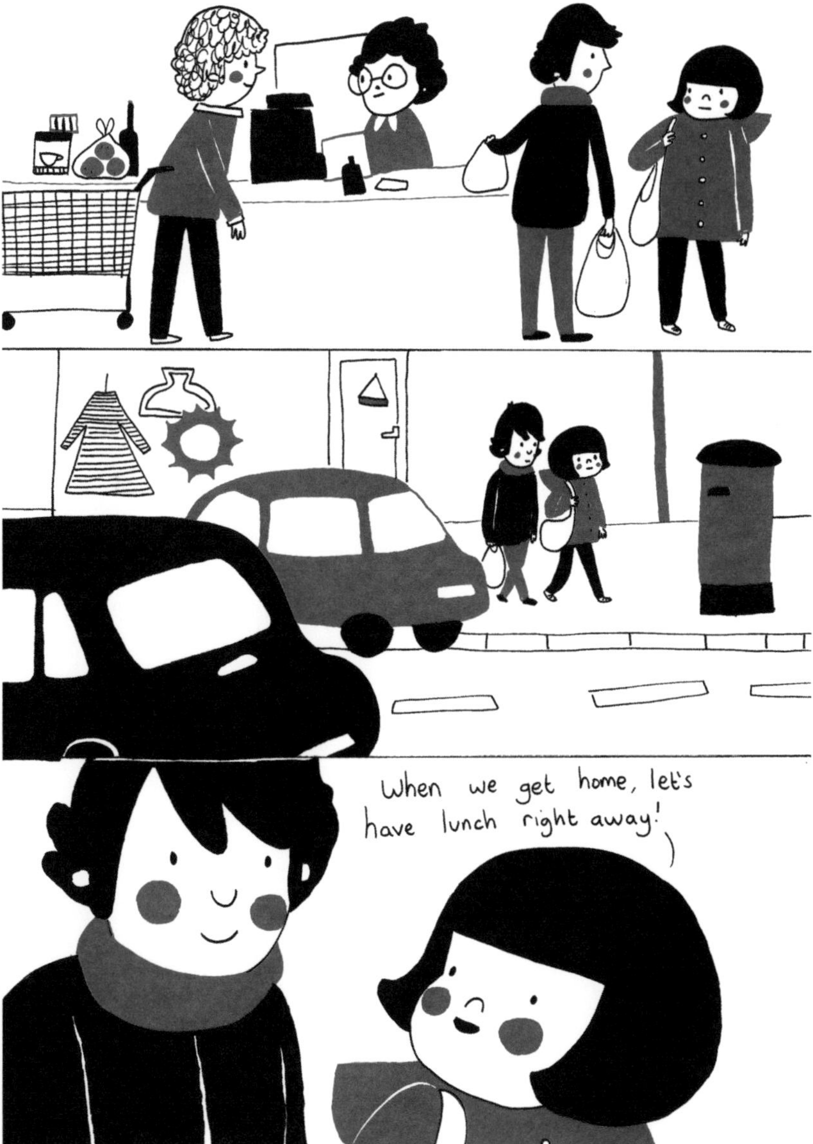
When we get home, let's have lunch right away!

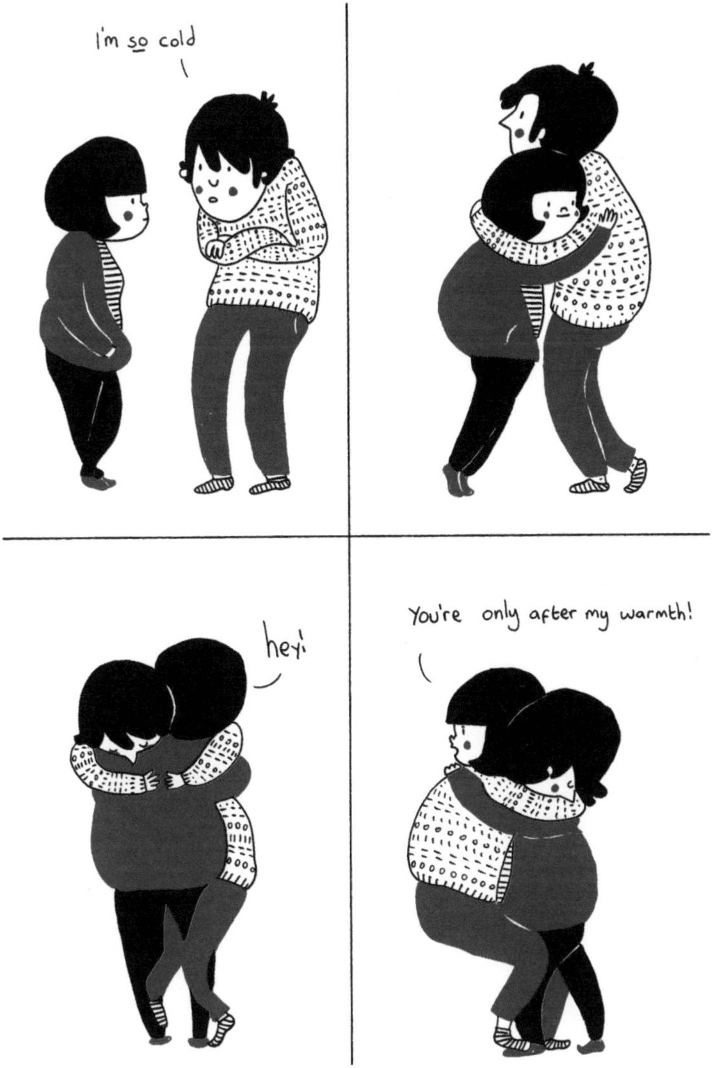
I'm so cold
hey!
You're only after my warmth!

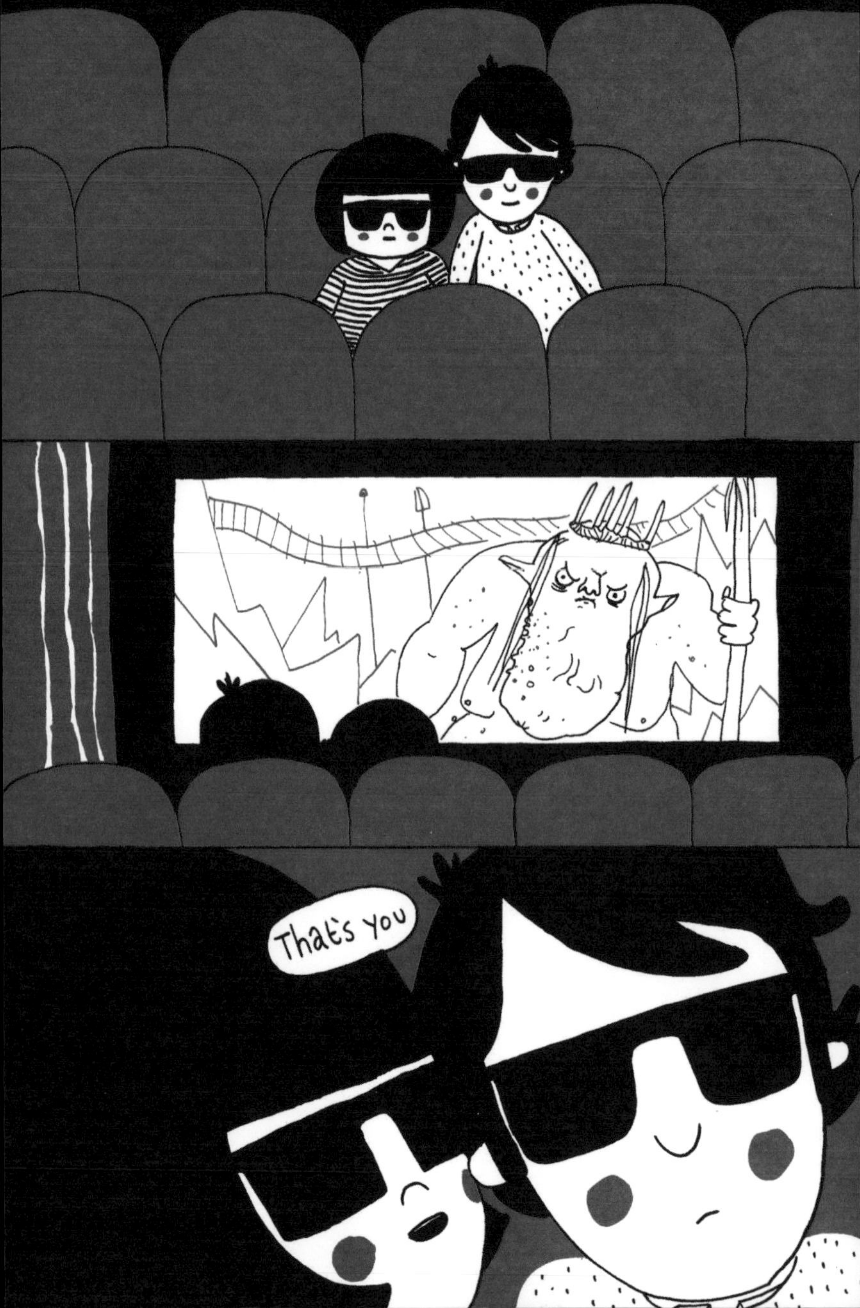
That's you

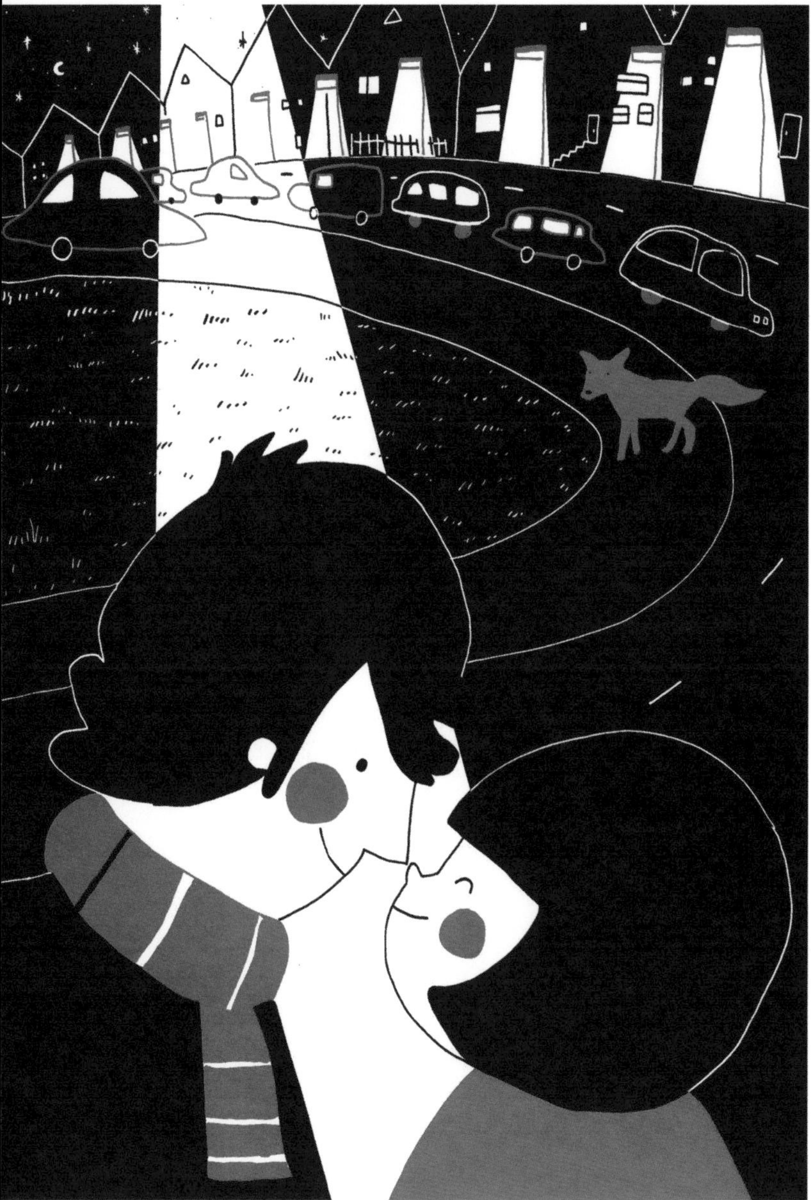

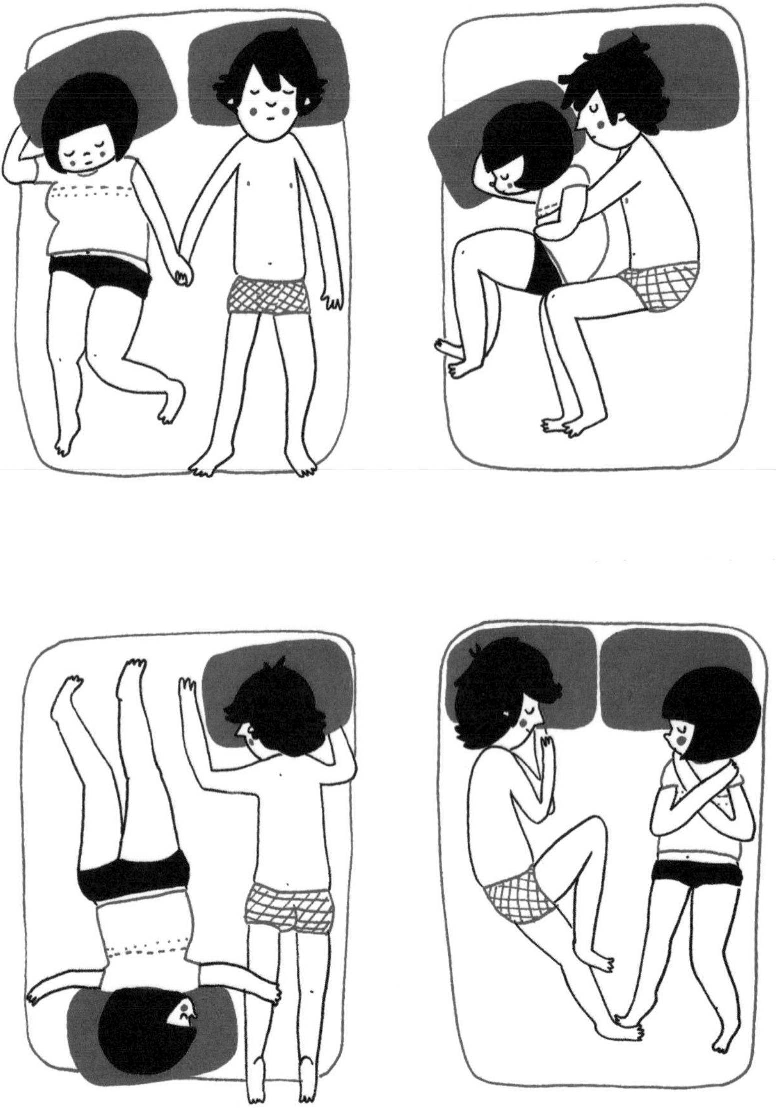

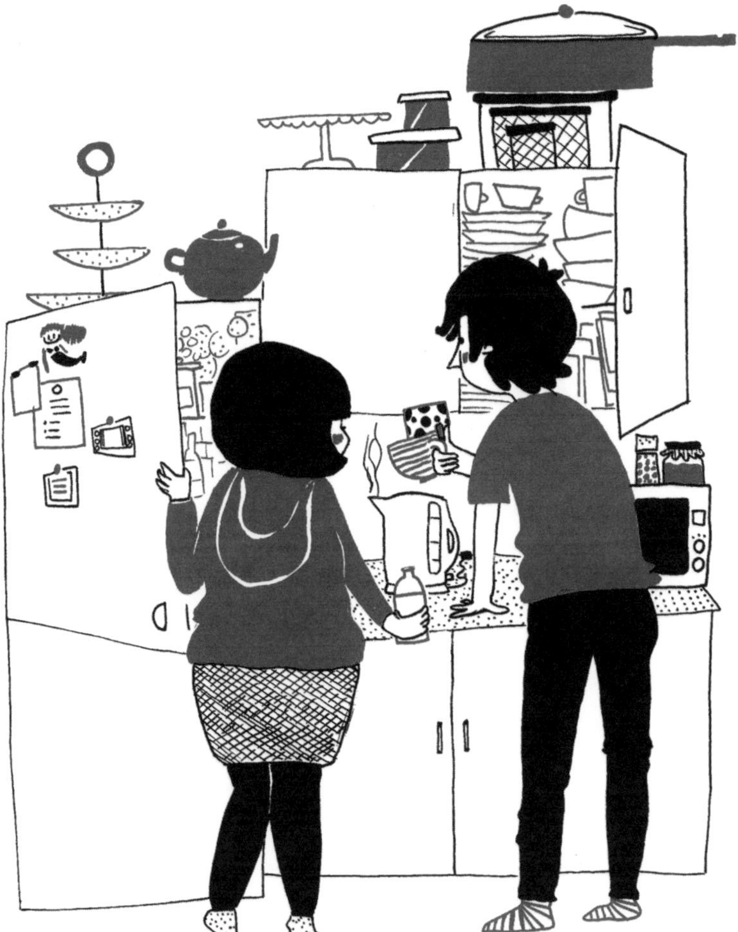

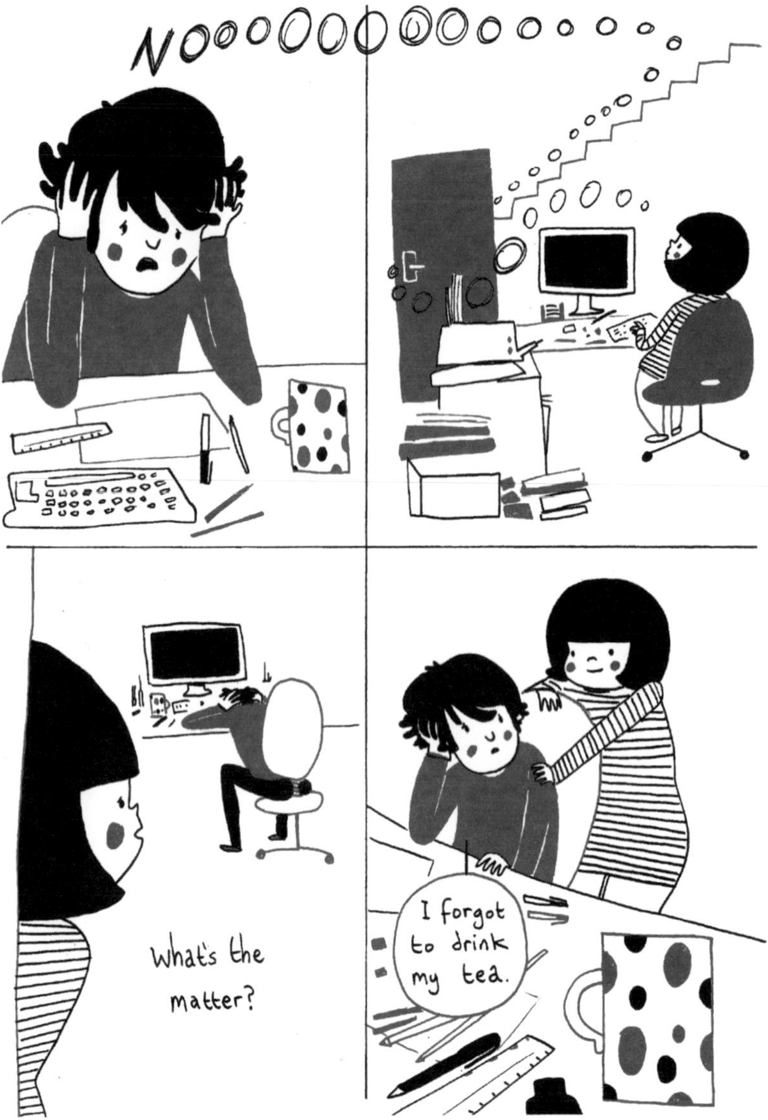
NOOOOOOOOOOOOOOOOooooo
What's the matter?
I forgot to drink my tea.

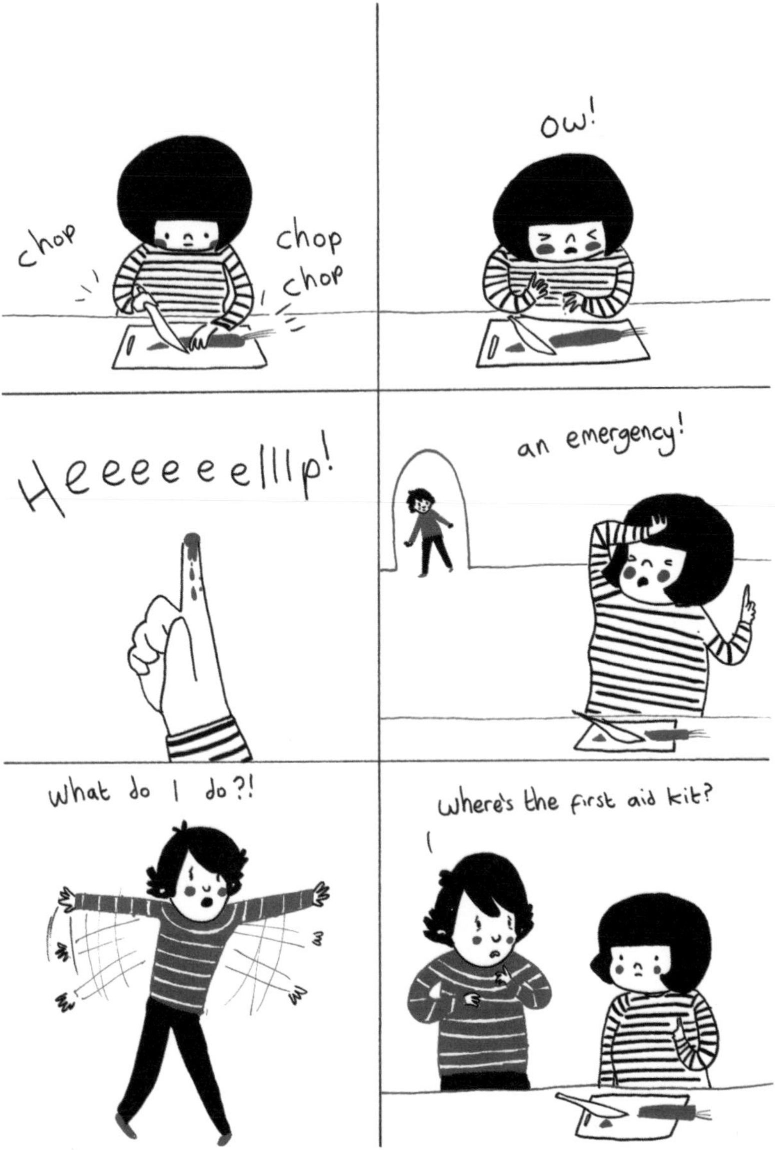
chop
chop
chop
ow!
Heeeeeelllp!
an emergency!
what do I do?!
where's the first aid kit?

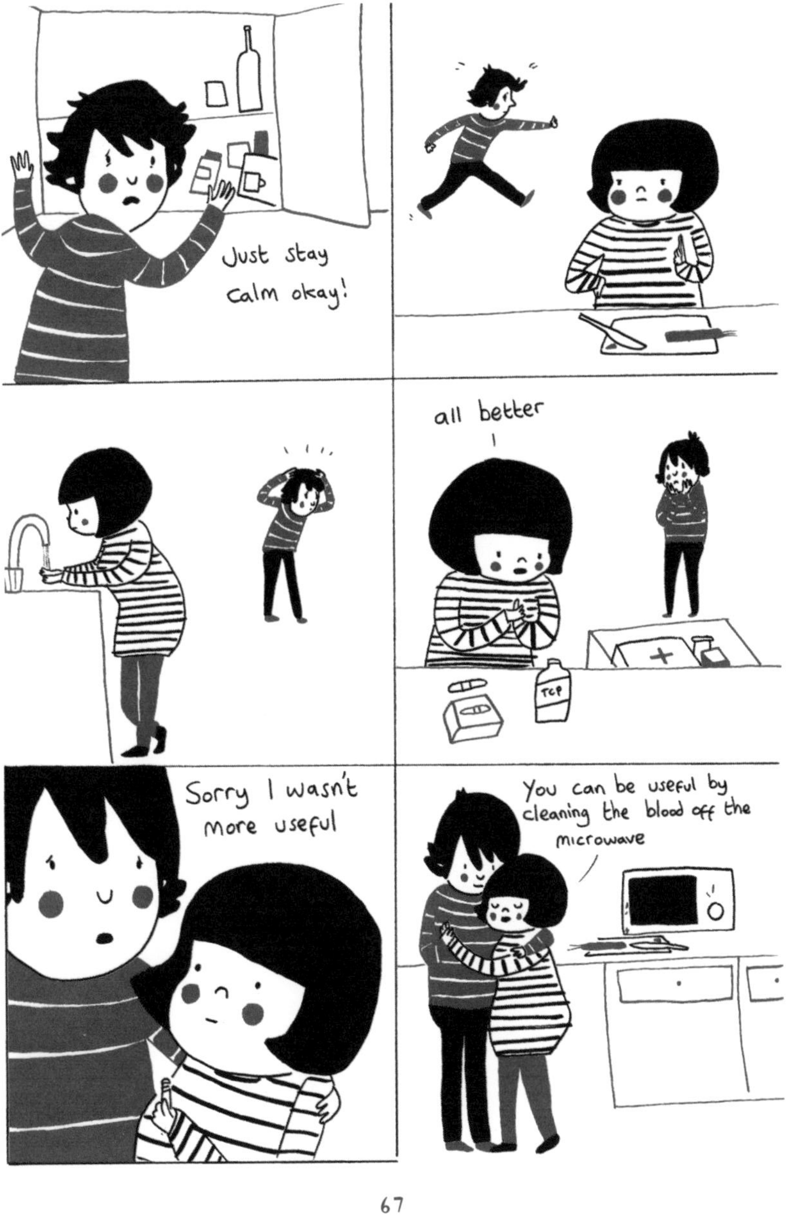
Just stay calm okay!
all better
Sorry I wasn't more useful
You can be useful by cleaning the blood off the microwave
TCP

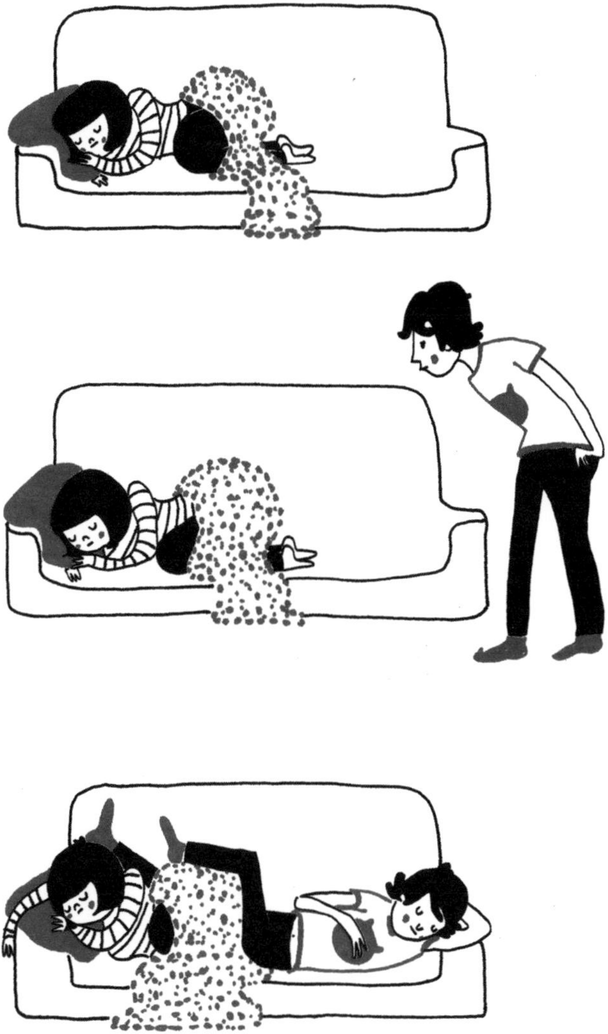

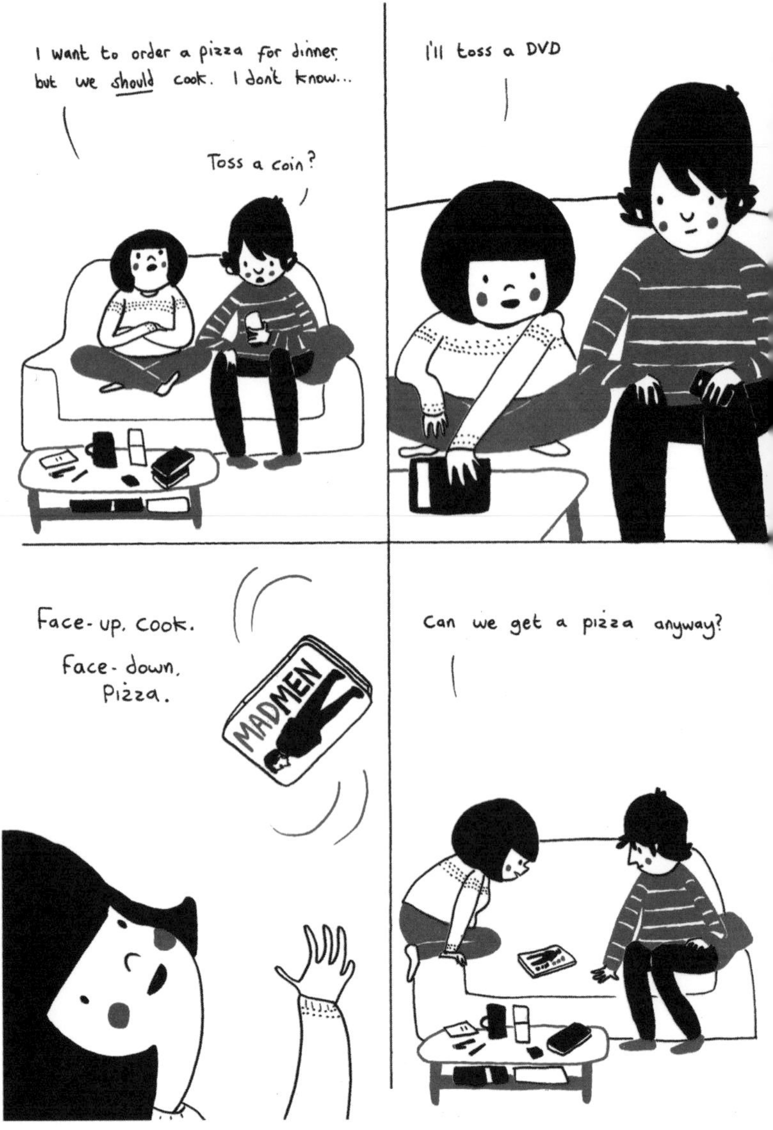
I want to order a pizza for dinner, but we should cook. I don't know...
Toss a coin?
I'll toss a DVD
Face-up, cook.
Face-down, Pizza.
MADMEN
Can we get a pizza anyway?

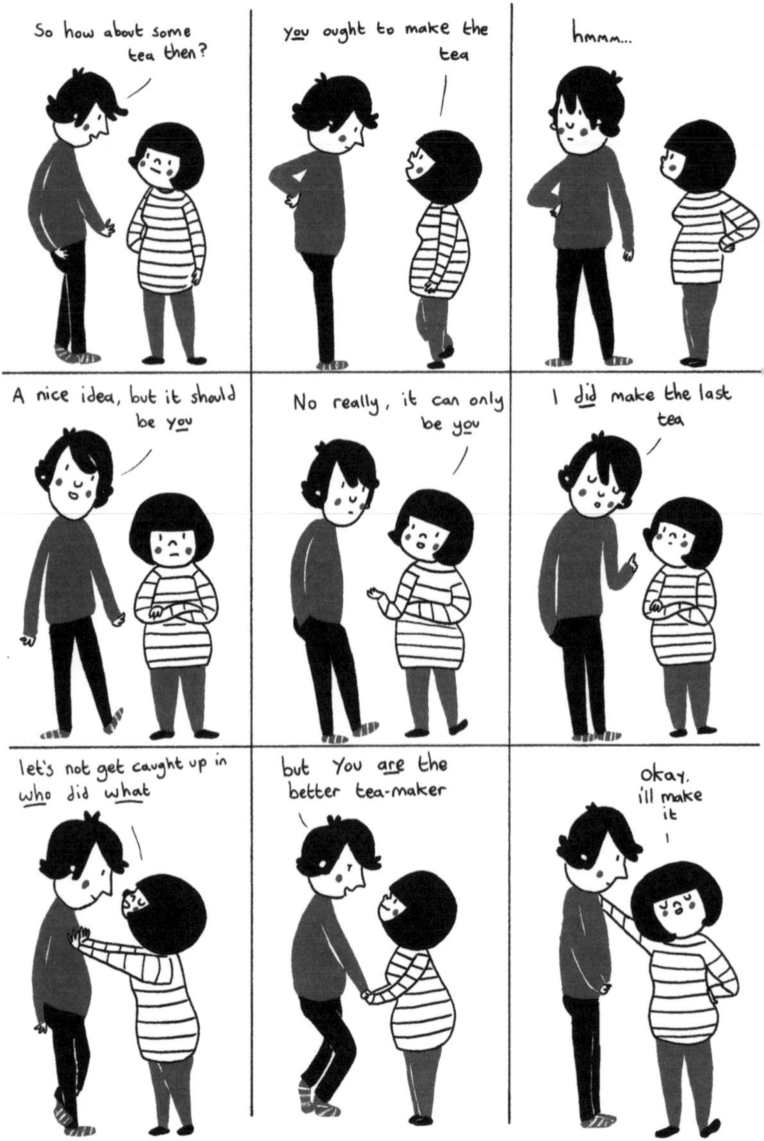

So how about some tea then?
you ought to make the tea
hmmm...
A nice idea, but it should be you
No really, it can only be you
I did make the last tea
let's not get caught up in who did what
but You are the better tea-maker
Okay. ill make it

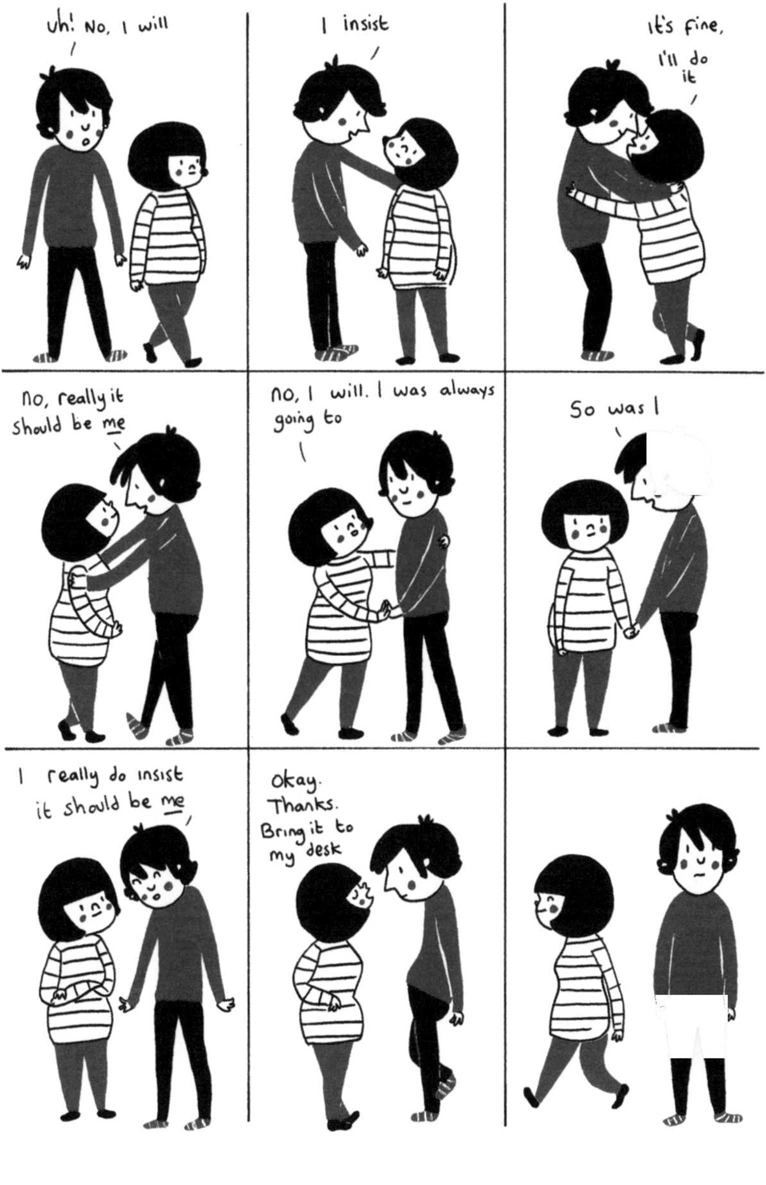

uh! No, I will
I insist
It's fine,
I'll do it
No, really it should be me
No, I will. I was always going to
So was I
I really do insist it should be me
Okay. Thanks. Bring it to my desk

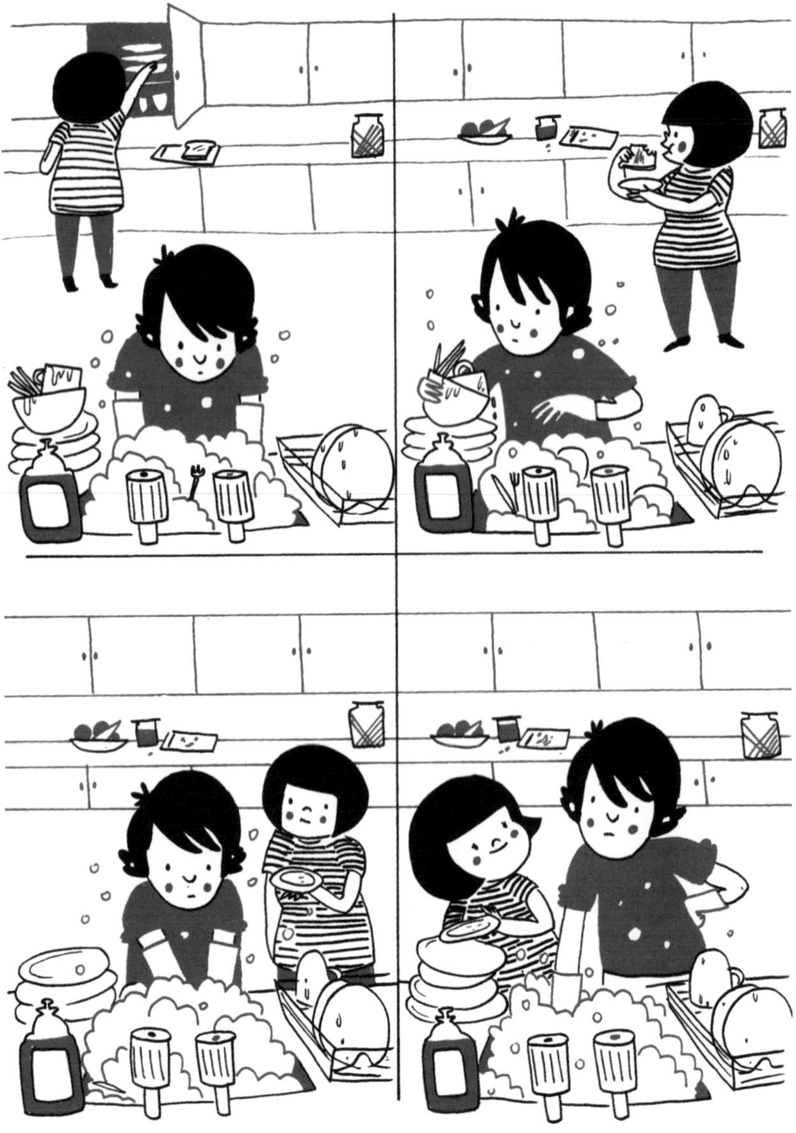

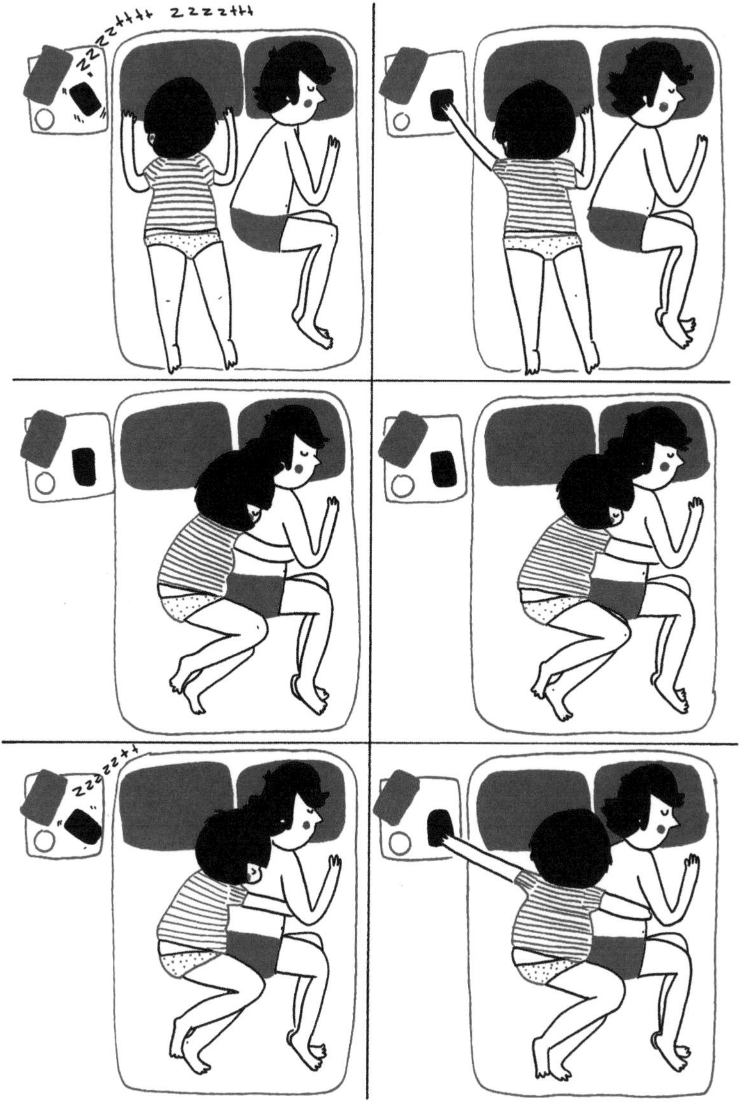
zzzzztttt zzzzttt
zzzzztt

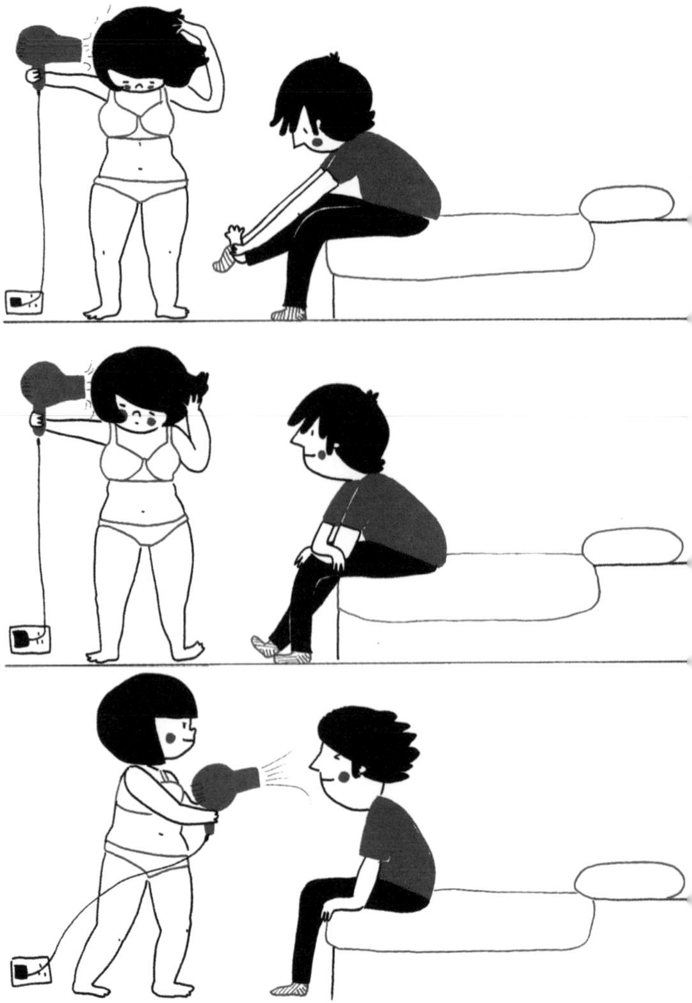

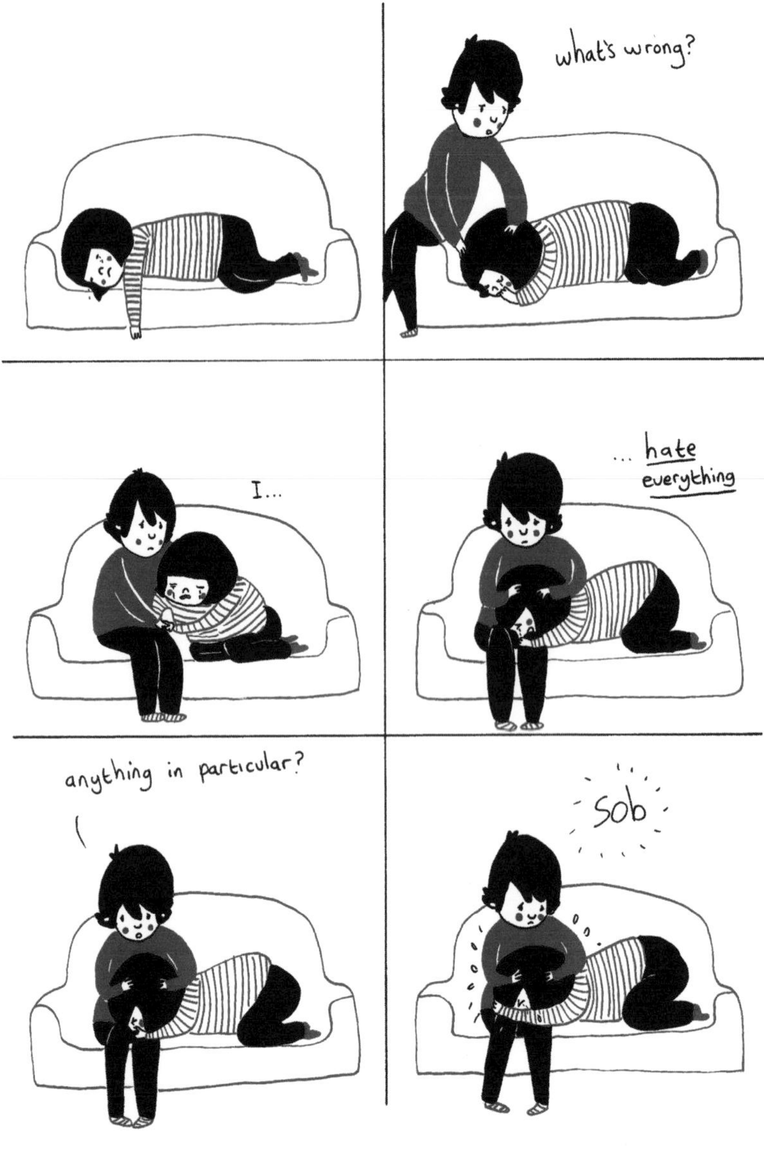
what's wrong?
I...
... hate everything
anything in particular?
Sob

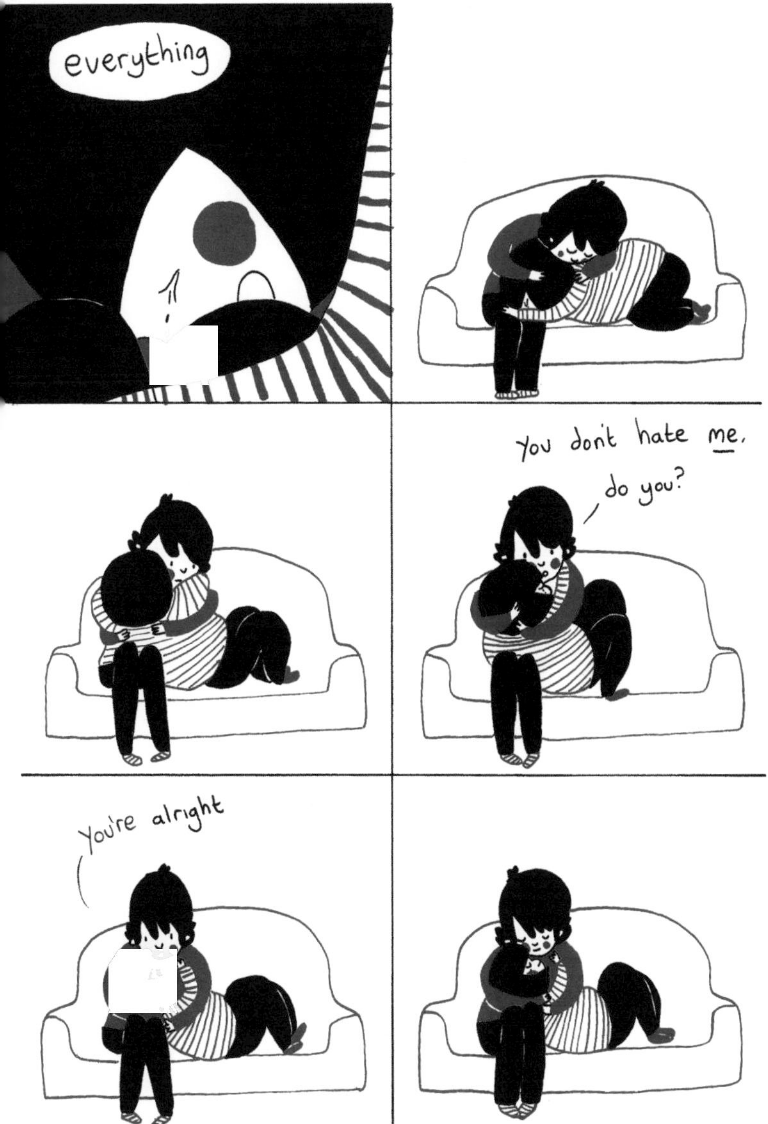
everything
You don't hate me, do you?
You're alright

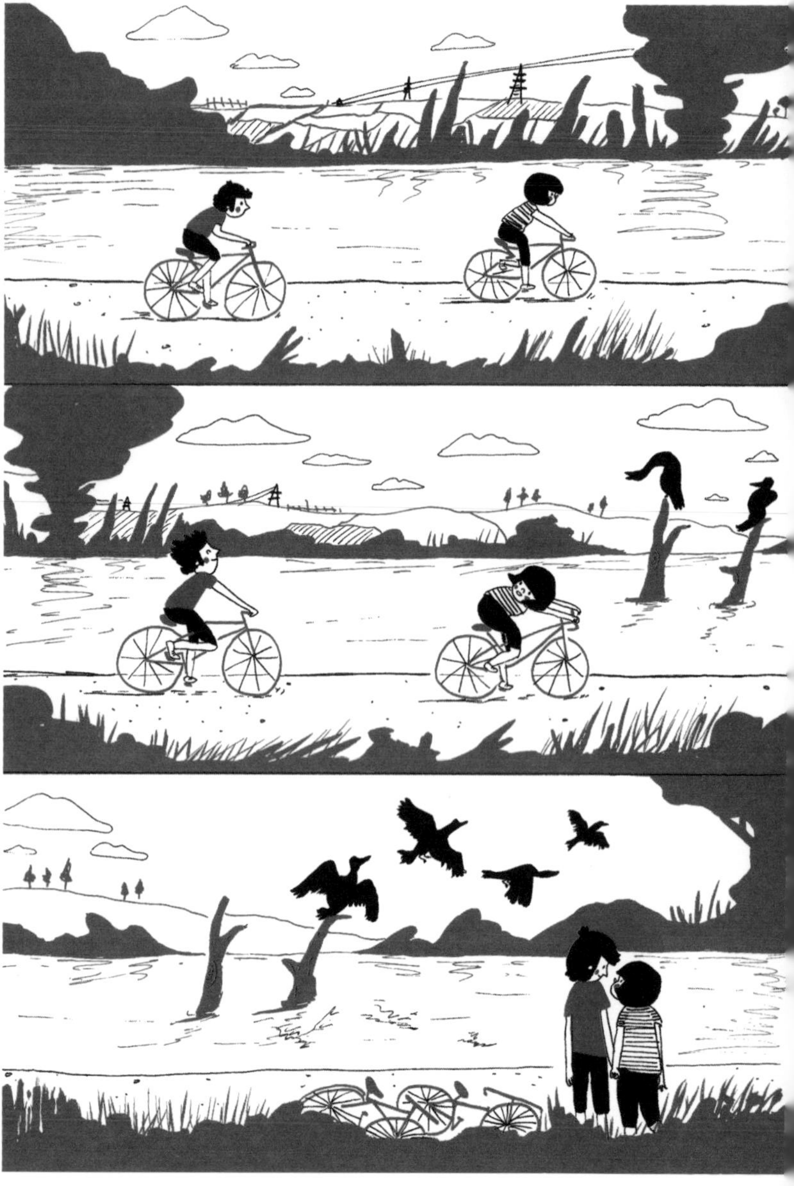

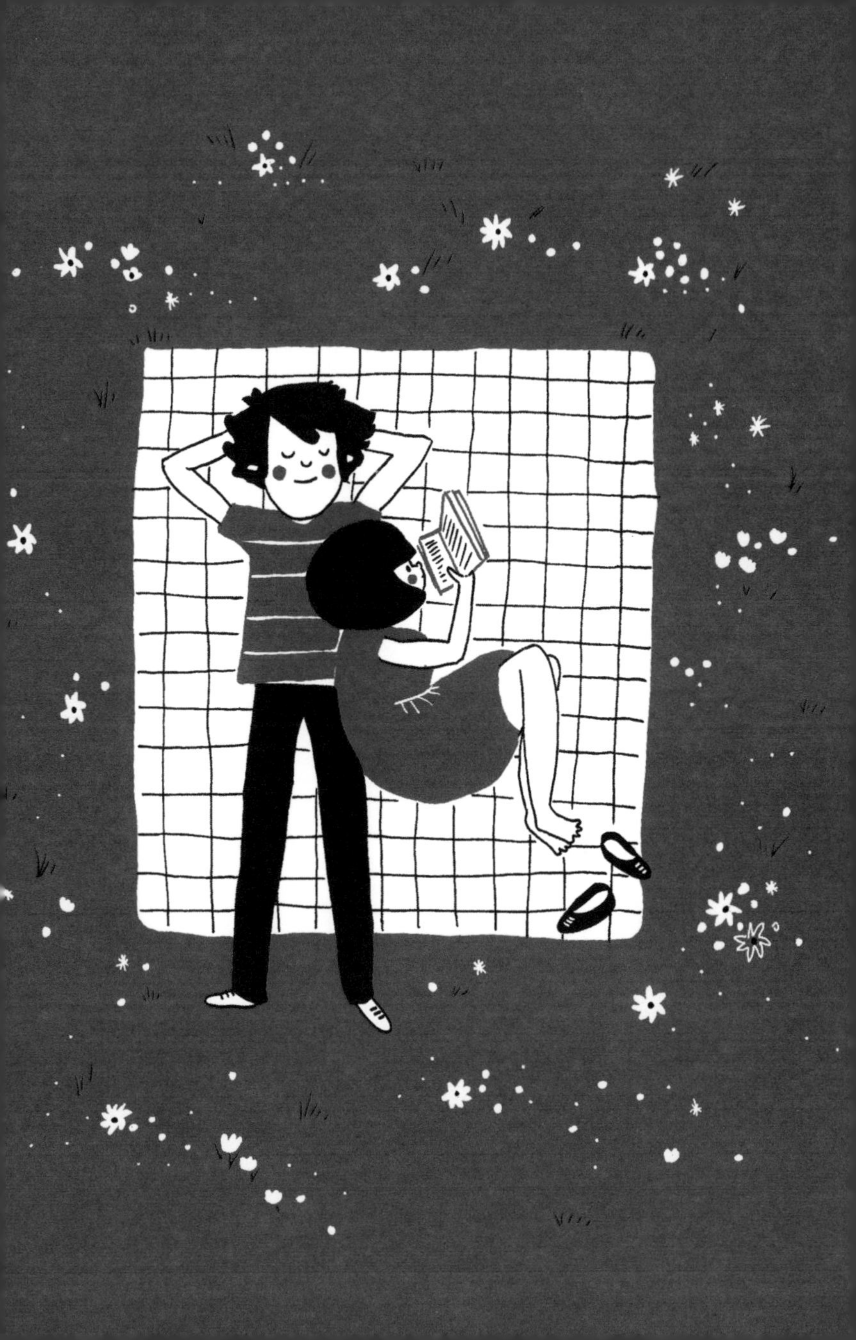

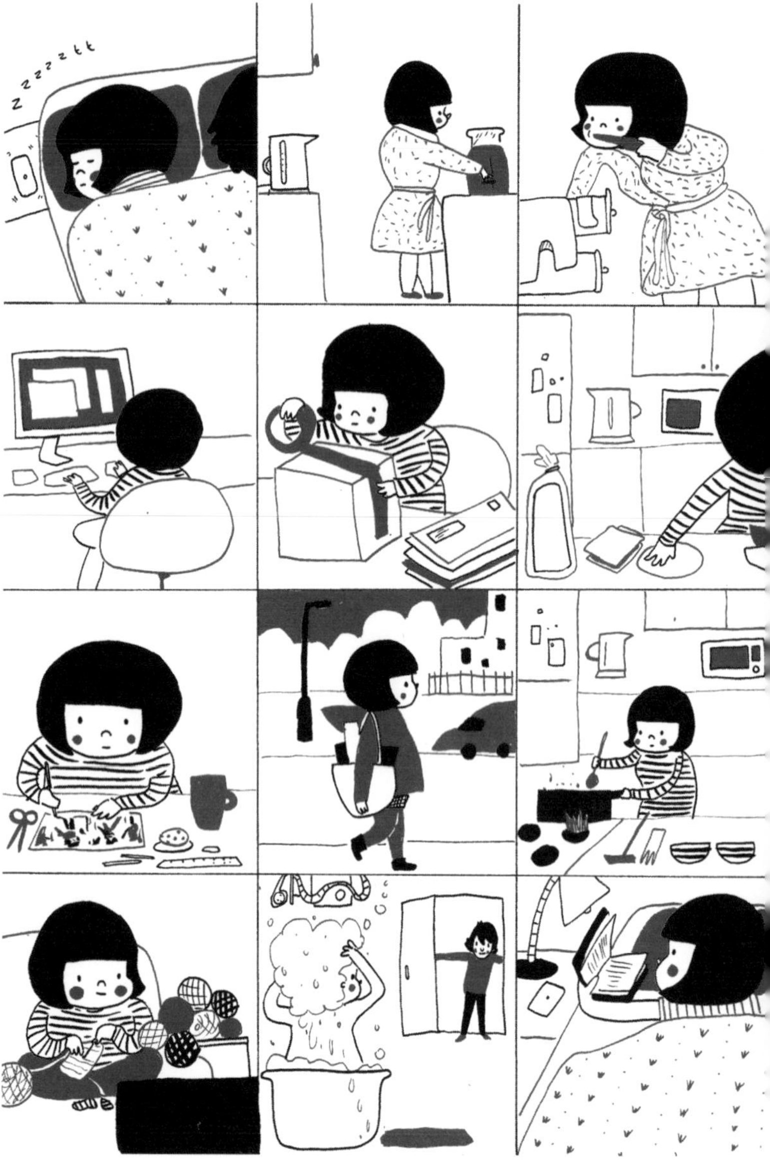
zzzzzkk

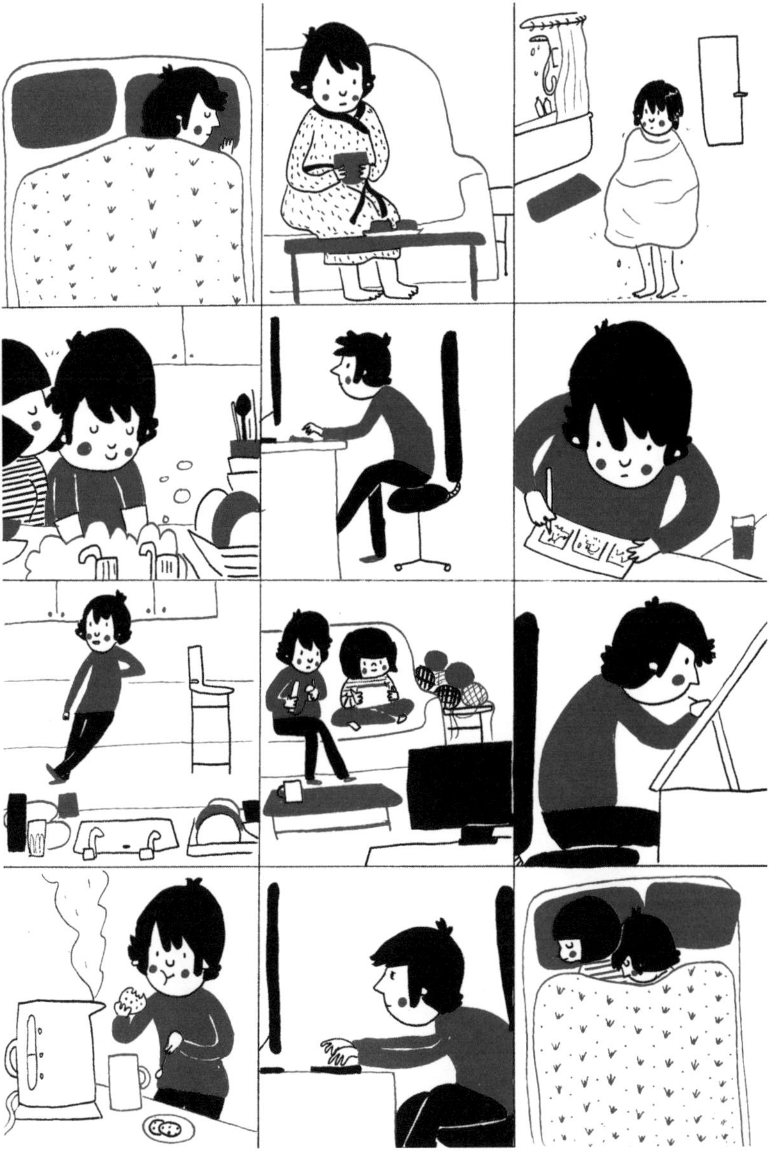

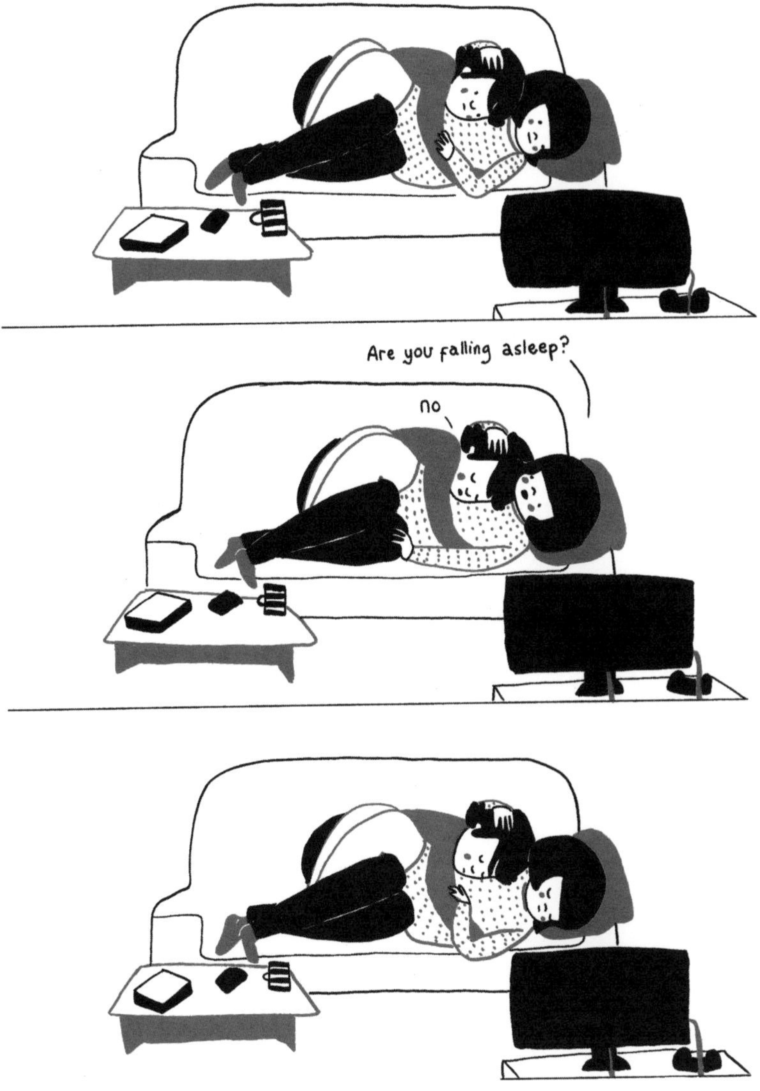
Are you falling asleep?
no

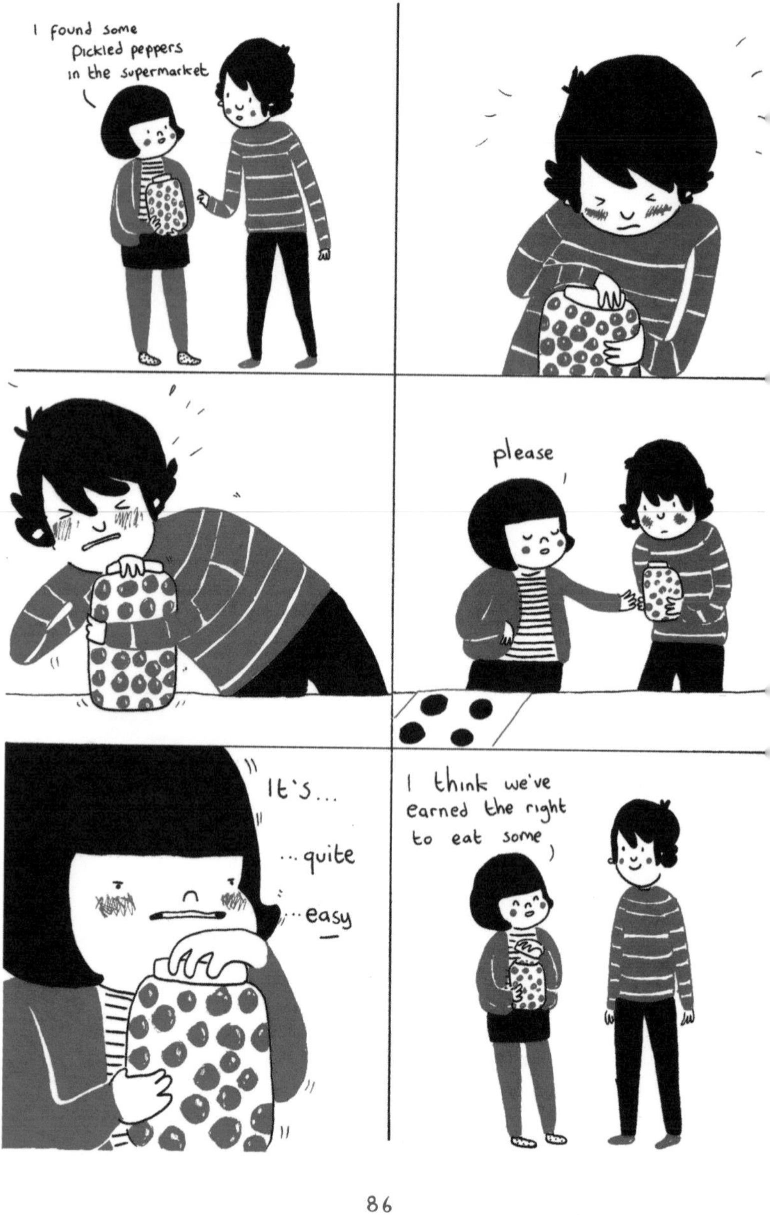
I found some pickled peppers in the supermarket
please
It's...
...quite
...easy
I think we've earned the right to eat some

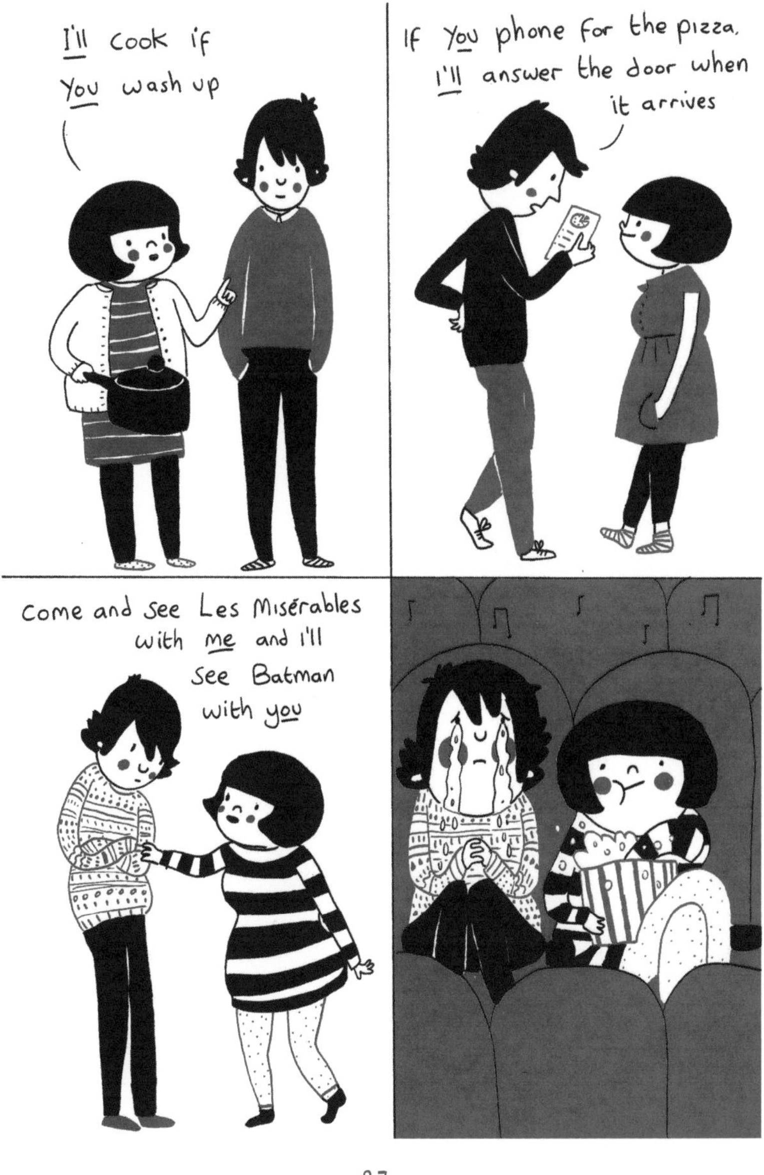
I'll cook if you wash up
If you phone for the pizza, I'll answer the door when it arrives
Come and see Les Misérables with me and I'll see Batman with you

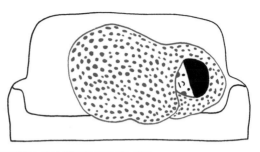

let me in!

No! Stop it! You're letting the cold in

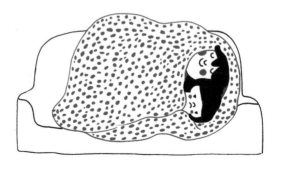

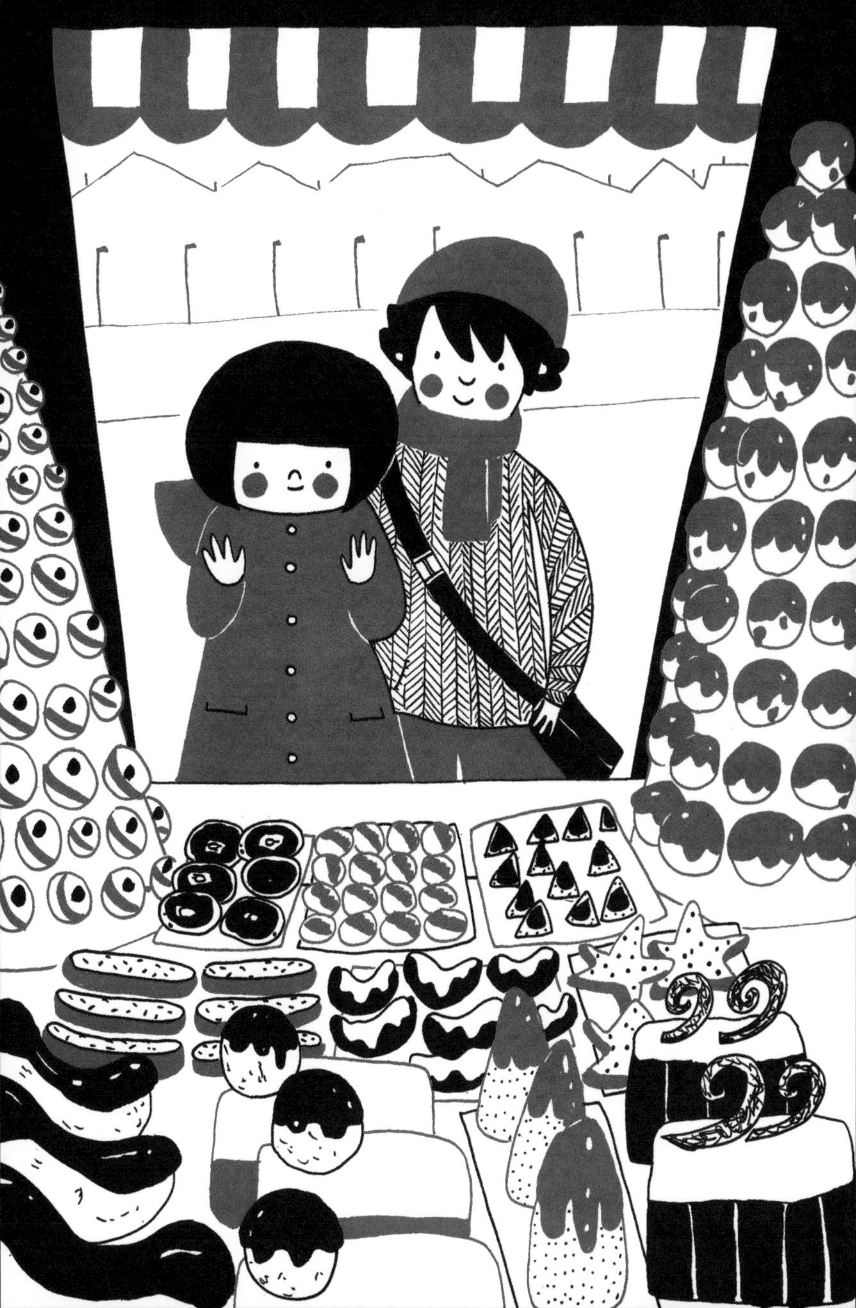

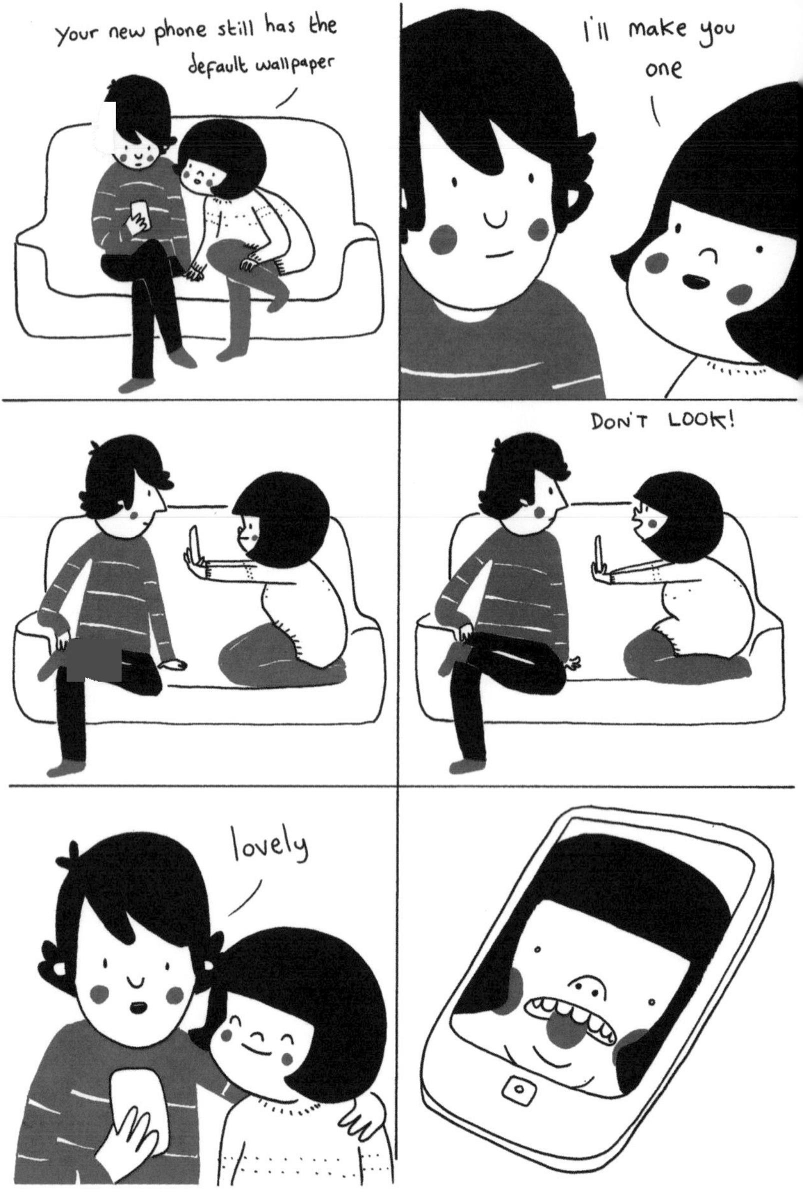
Your new phone still has the default wallpaper
I'll make you one
DON'T LOOK!
lovely

92

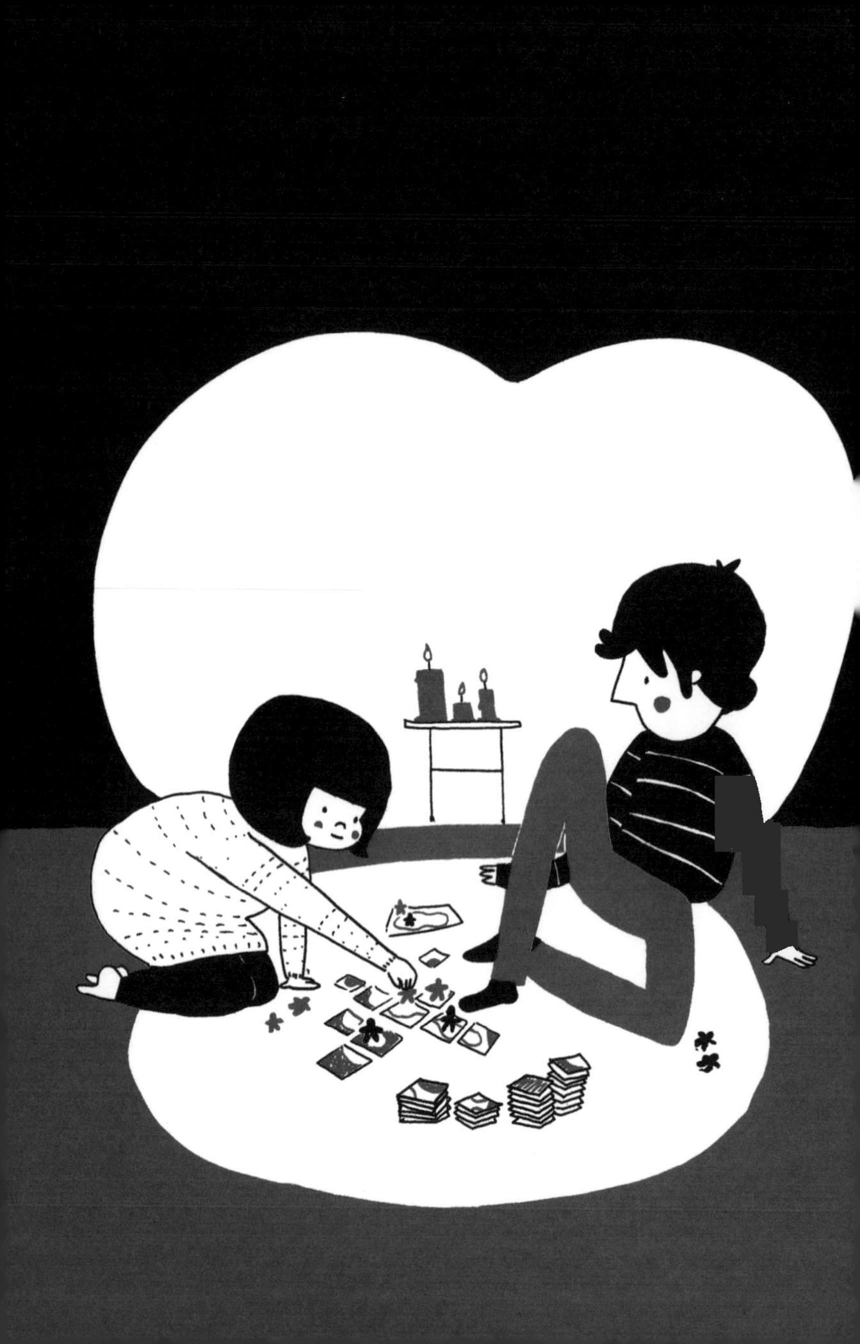

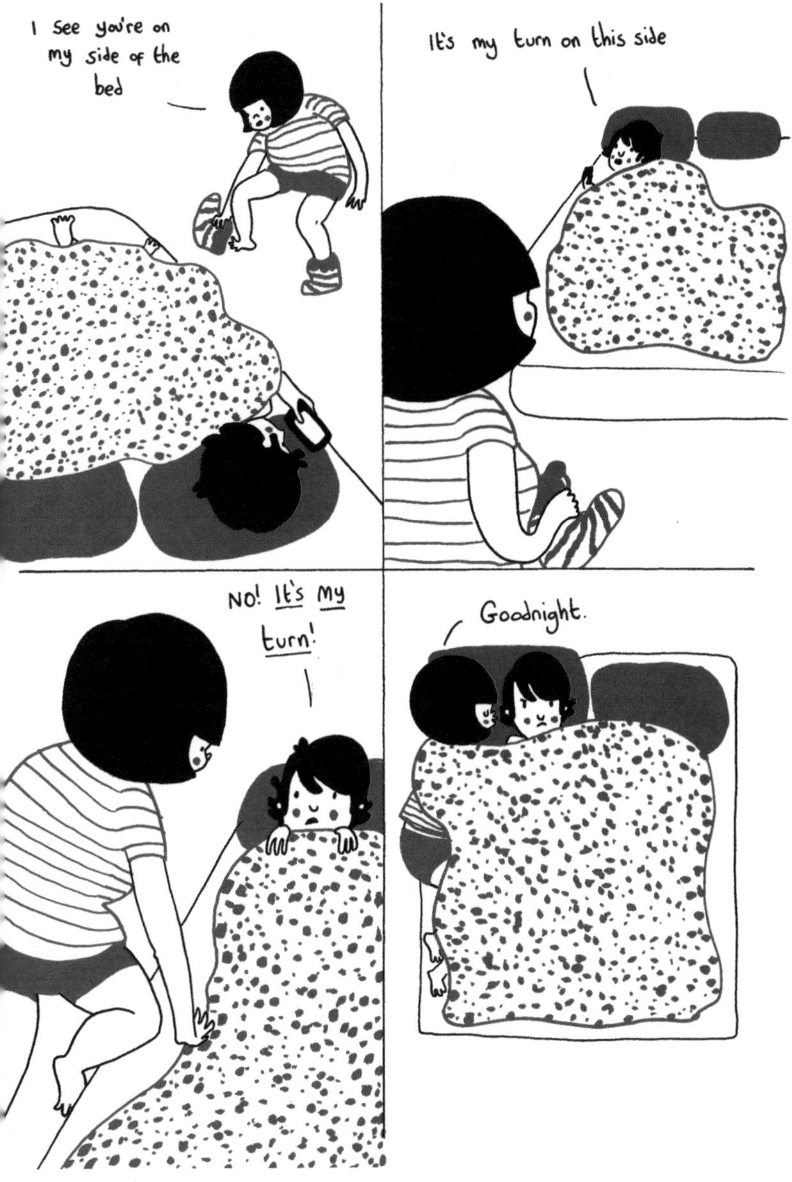
I see you're on my side of the bed
It's my turn on this side
No! It's my turn!
Goodnight.

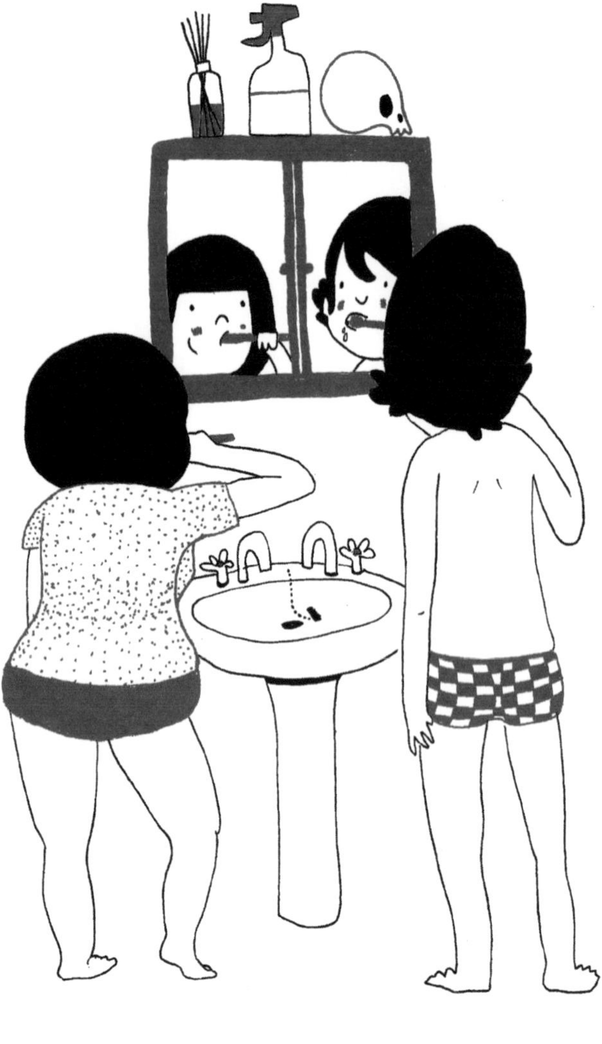

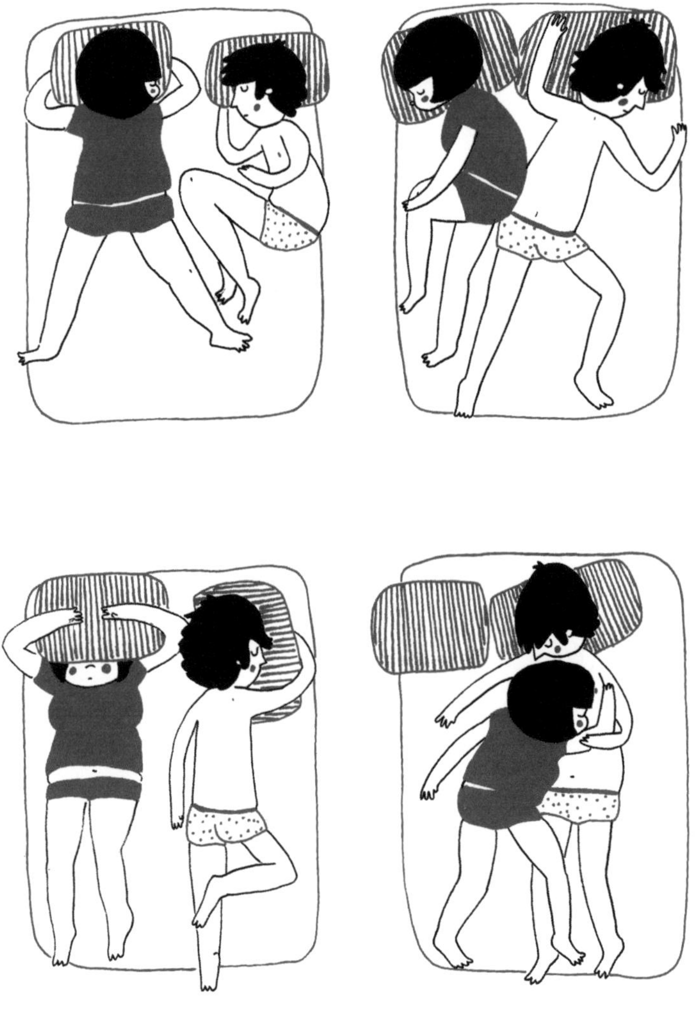

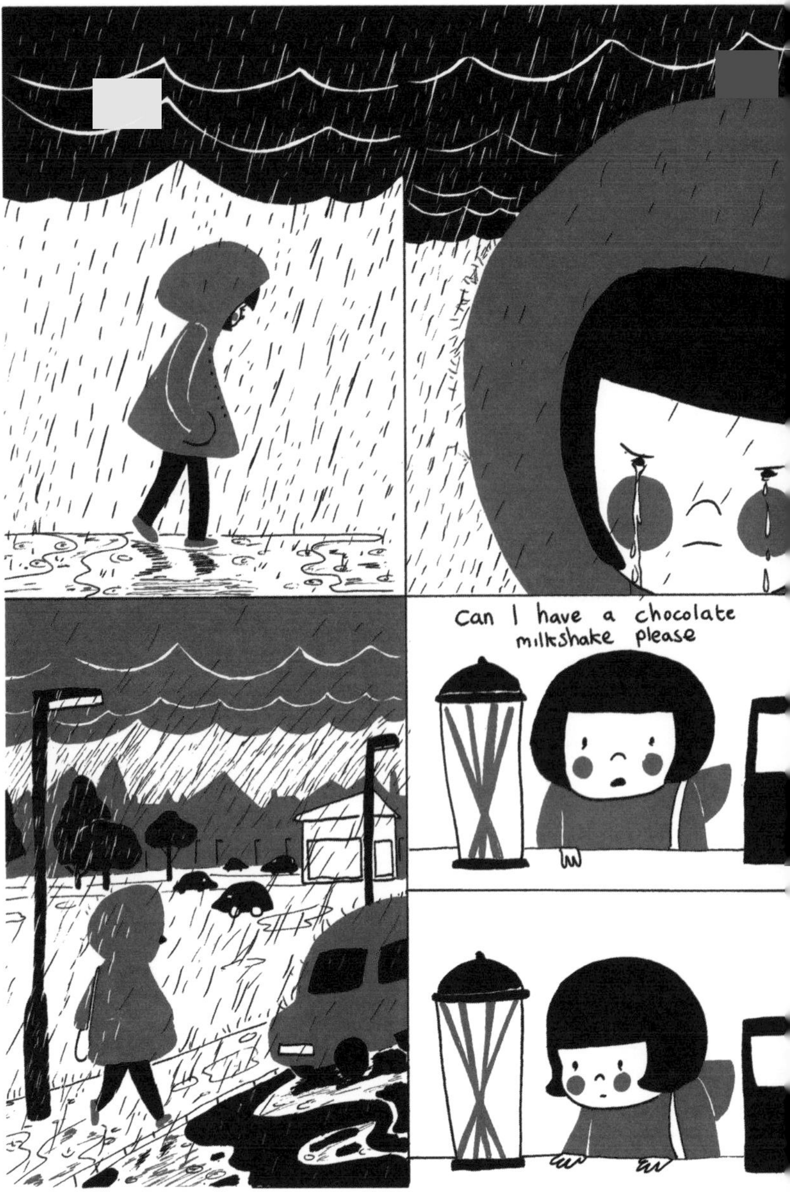
Can I have a chocolate milkshake please

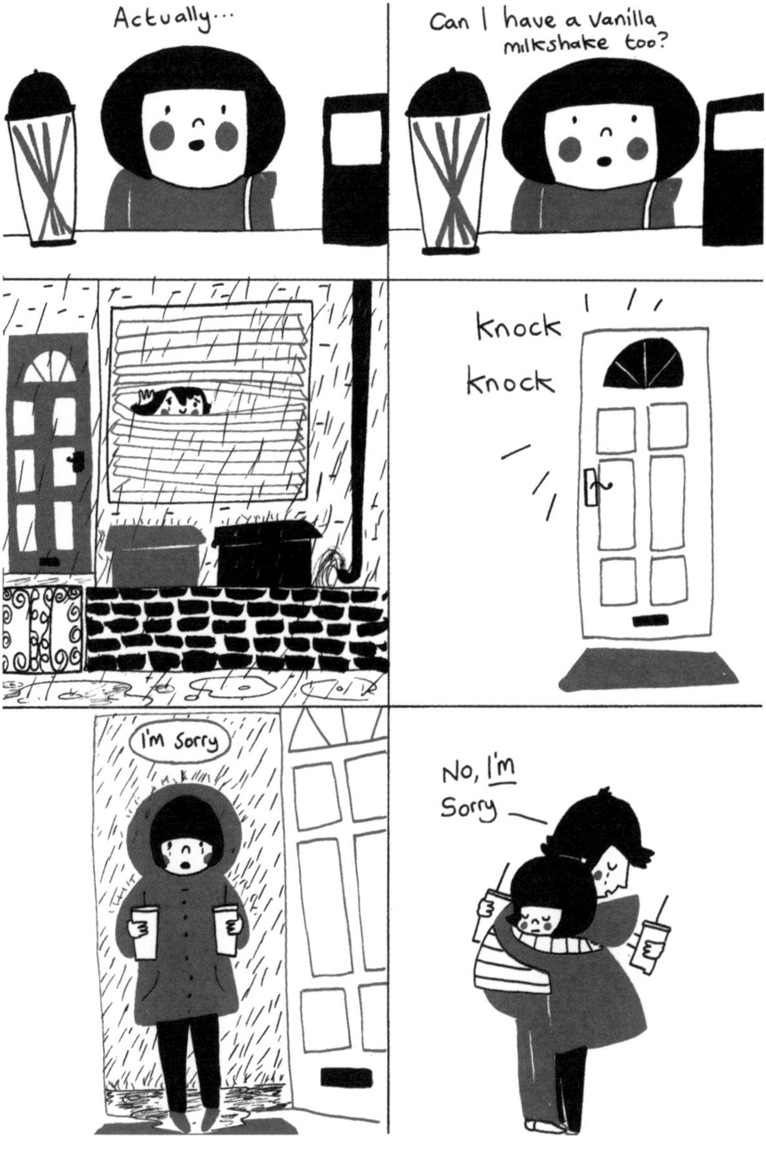
Actually...
Can I have a vanilla milkshake too?
knock
knock
I'm sorry
No, I'm sorry

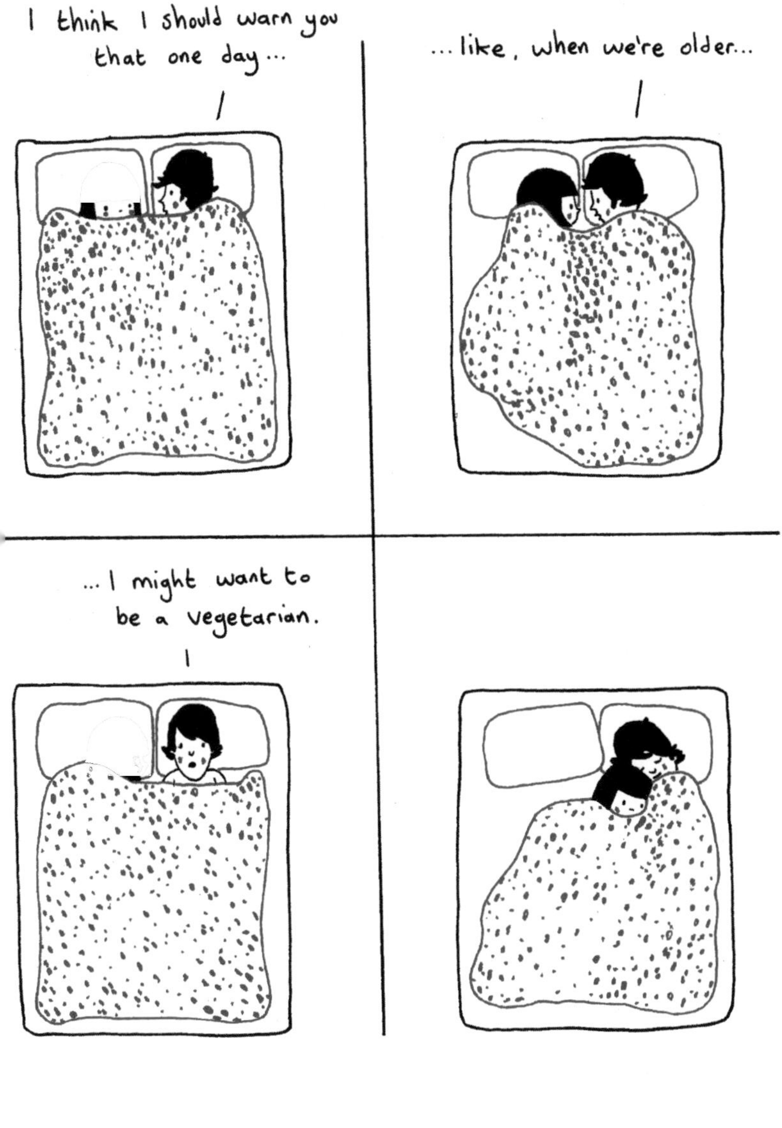
I think I should warn you that one day...
...like, when we're older...
...I might want to be a vegetarian.

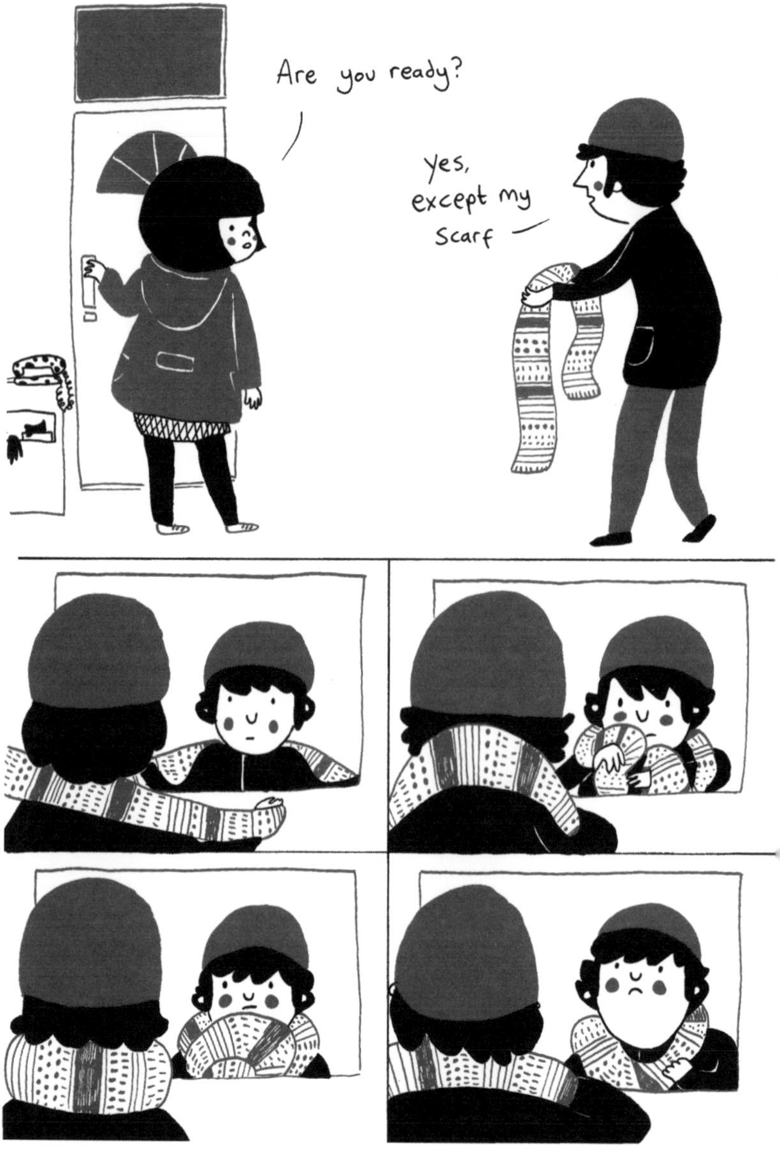
Are you ready?
yes, except my scarf

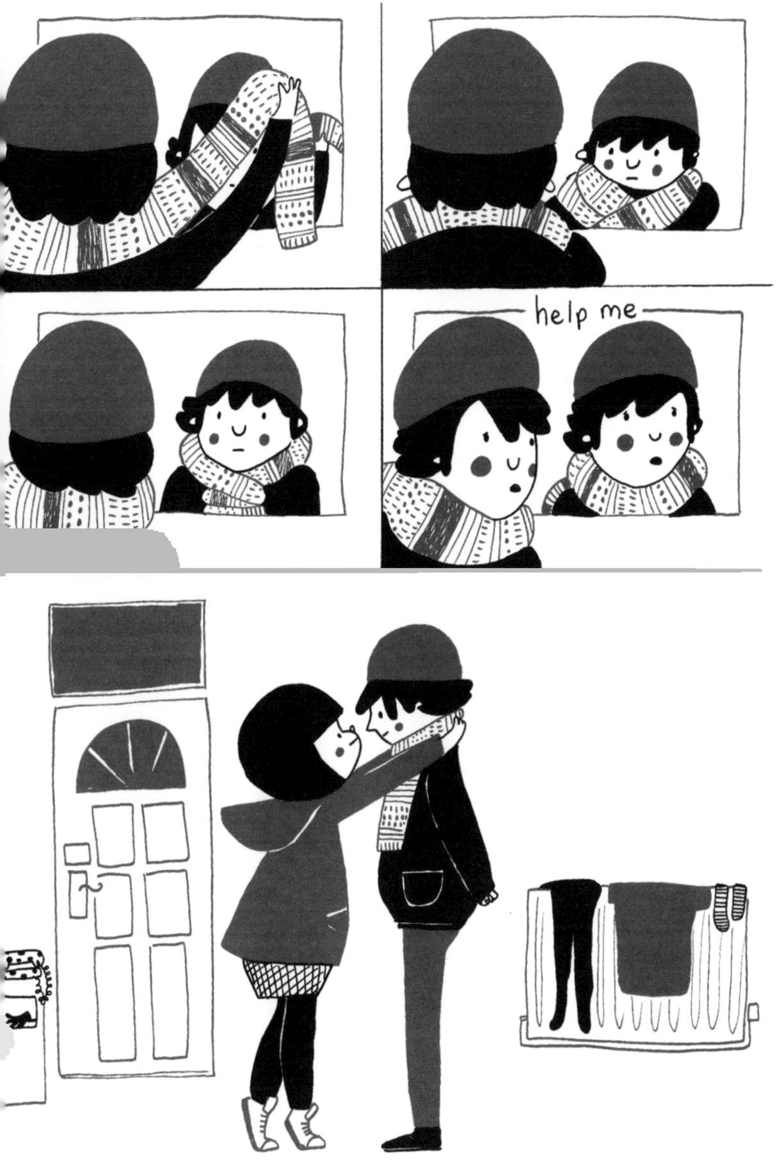
help me

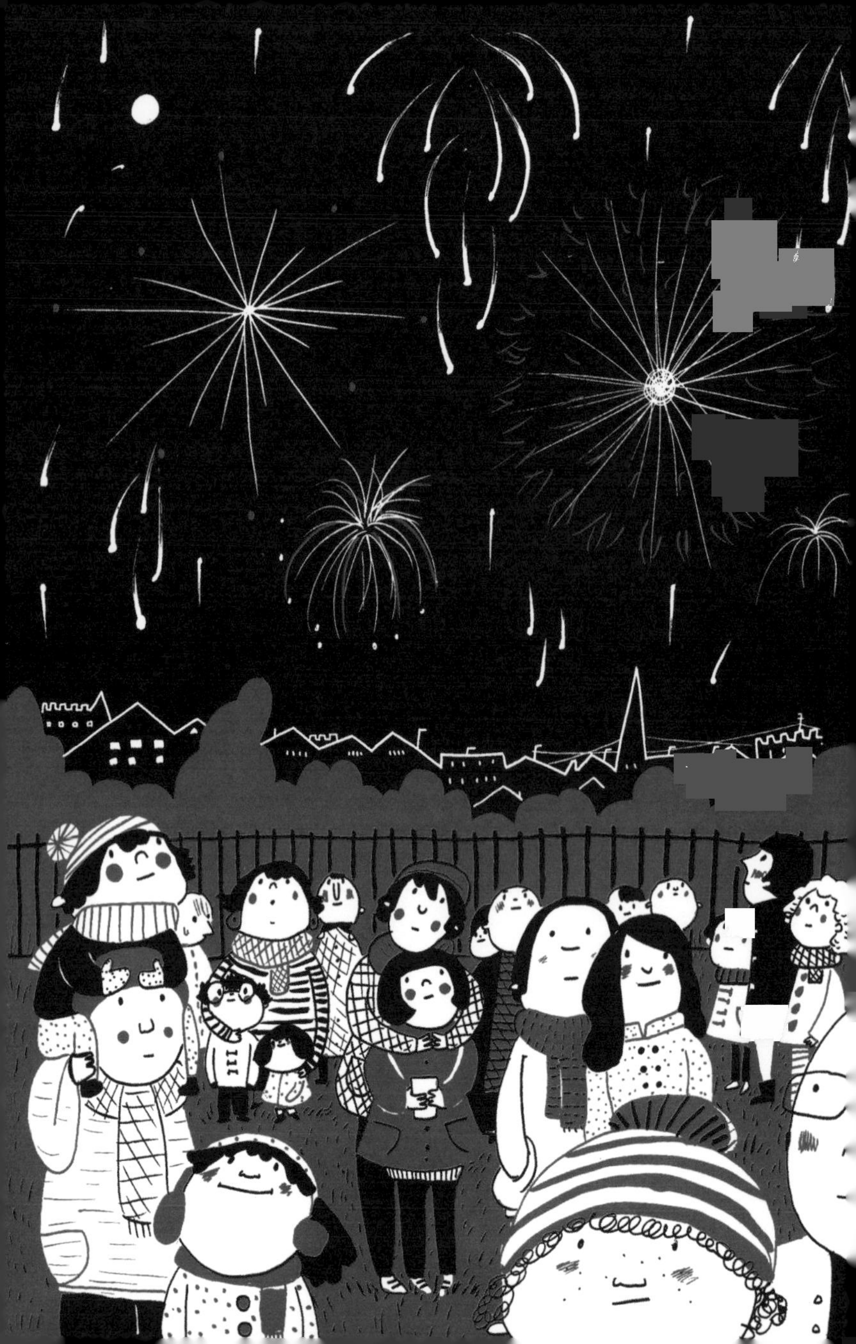

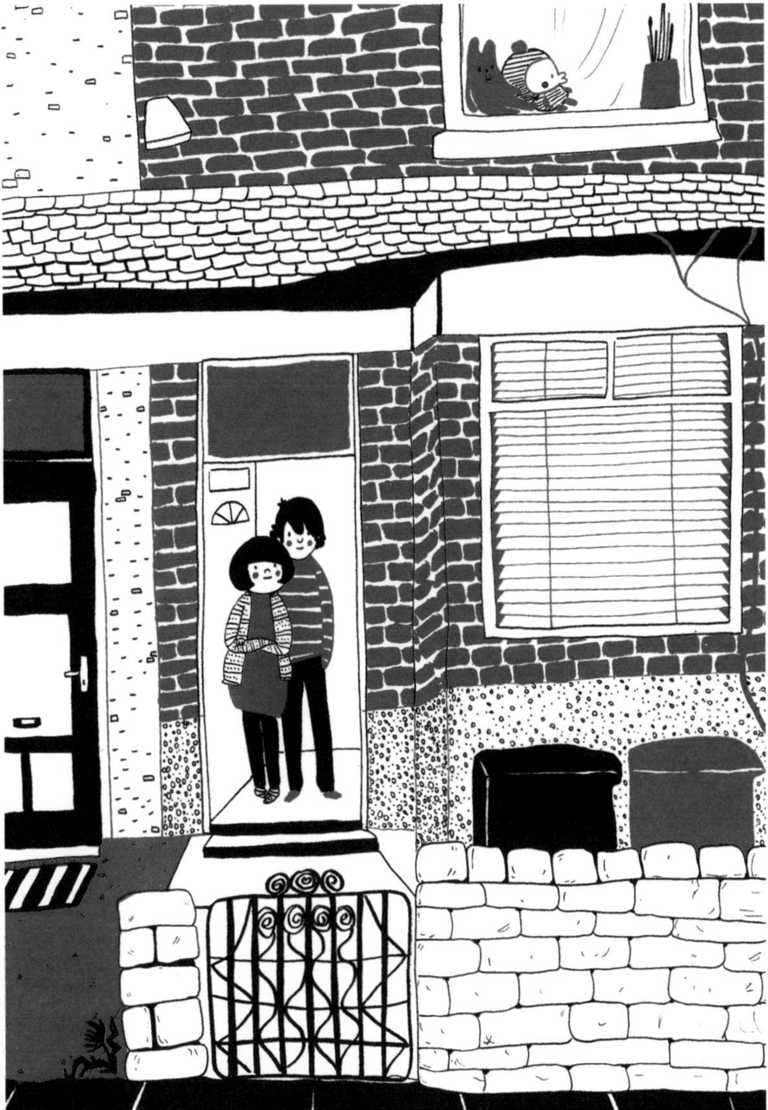

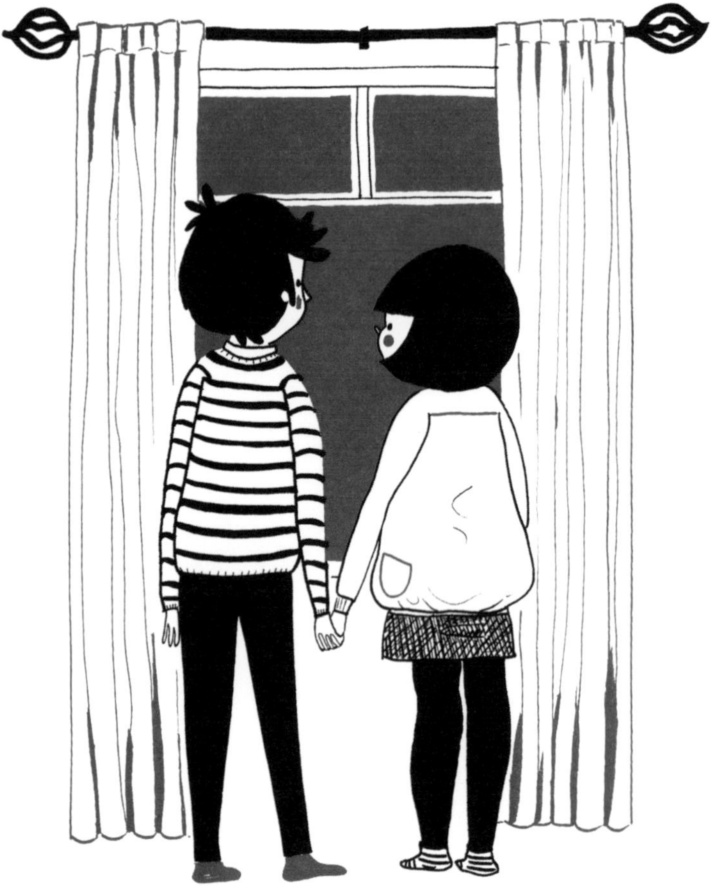

Philippa Rice is an artist who works in a number of different mediums including comics, illustration, animation, model-making and crochet. Her other works include the collage based webcomic, *My Cardboard Life* and her stop-motion animated characters.

Philippa grew up in London and now she lives in Nottingham with illustrator Luke Pearson.

Andrews McMeel Publishing
a division of Andrews McMeel Universal
1130 Walnut Street, Kansas City, Missouri 64106

www.andrewsmcmeel.com

16 17 18 19 20 TEN 10 9 8 7 6 5 4

ISBN: 978-1-4494-6106-5

Library of Congress Control Number: 2014940304

ATTENTION: SCHOOLS AND BUSINESSES

Andrews McMeel books are available at quantity discounts with bulk
purchase for educational, business, or sales promotional use.
For information, please e-mail the Andrews McMeel Publishing
Special Sales Department: specialsales@amuniversal.com.